DREAMS
COME TRUE

DREAMS
COME TRUE

DISCOVERING GOD'S VISION
FOR YOUR LIFE

JAMES R. WALTERS

New City Press
Hyde Park, New York

Published by New City Press
202 Comforter Blvd.,
Hyde Park, NY 12538
www.newcitypress.com

Cover design and layout by Miguel Tejerina
Back cover photo by Jad Nammour

Library of Congress Cataloging-in-Publication Data
Dreams Come True

Library of Congress Control Number: 2020931317

ISBN 978-1-56548-008-7 (paperback)
ISBN 978-1-56548-011-7 (e-book)

Printed in the United States of America

CONTENTS

ACKNOWLEDGMENTS

My heartfelt gratitude...

To the talented and dedicated team at New City Press for making this dream come true, especially Claude Blanc; Gary Brandl; Nick Cianfarani; Greg Metzger; and Matteo Pota. A special thank you to my editor, Tom Masters for sharing his talents with me and the world.

To my students who inspire and challenge me, who reveal the face of God, and who trust me to accompany them on their journey.

To the Catholic Scholars, for providing hope for our world—you truly are "Light of the World."

To Dr. Conrado Gempesaw; Rev. Bernard Tracey, C.M.; and all those in leadership at St. John's University for the opportunity to lead and minister to our community.

To my past and present friends and colleagues in Campus Ministry, for inspiring me to serve our campus with faith, justice, and love, especially James Behan; Jordan Bouchard; Tom Donoghue; Joseph Gagliano; Dennis Gallagher; Kate Giancatarino; Patrick Gordon; Norm Gouin; Cydni Joubert; Dr. Widian Nicola; Victoria O'Keefe; Andrea Pinnavaia; Meg Rodriguez; Scott Salvato; Trish Scalese; Ketienne Telemaque; Pat Tracey; Mary Scholfield; and many more too numerous to mention.

To Lilliana Bruschi; Stephen DeBlasio; Paula Migliore; and Sr. Pat Evanick, D.C. for your very special friendship, support, and sharing of life and ministry.

To Tori Santangelo for your incredible leadership, friendship, love of ministry, and dedication and consistent support in bringing this book to fruition.

To Dr. Angela Seegel for your friendship, care and support, and always providing valuable perspective!

To Dr. Pamela Shea-Byrnes for your leadership, witness, mentorship, and friendship—even from the other side.

To Bro. Mike Sheerin, F.M.S., for your witness of pastoral ministry, your endless support, and your decades worth of spiritual guidance and wisdom that helped inspire this book.

To my present and former colleagues at St. John's University, especially Dr. Chris Cuccia; Dr. Andrew Ferdinandi; Christine Goodwin; Dr. Jacqueline Grogan; Dr. Joann Heaney-Hunter; Dr. Kathryn Hutchinson; Dr. Nancy Kaplan; Jackie Lochrie; Nunzia Manuli; Jad Nammour; Dr. Andre McKenzie; Kathy Meehan; Lucy Pesce; Dr. Rene Parmar; and Dot Schmitt.

To Rev. Dennis Holtschneider, C.M., and the Association of Catholic Colleges and Universities for their trust in awarding an early grant as I started my research with Appreciative Inquiry and Catholic faith formation, setting the groundwork for this book.

To Dr. Mike St. Pierre and the Catholic Campus Ministry Association for your support and leadership in the Church and Higher Education.

To Dr. Jennifer Bloom and her team for welcoming me into the Appreciative Education Family.

To my Vincentian family for the trust and invitation to join their mission of knowing and serving those most in need, especially Rev. Joe Agostino, C.M.; Rev. Michael Carroll, C.M.; Rev. Kevin Creagh, C.M.; Rev. Joseph Daly C.M.; Rev. Tri Duong, C.M.; Rev. Patrick Flanagan, C.M.; Rev. John Freund, C.M.; Sr. Nora Gatto, D.C.; Rev. Greg Gay, C.M.; Rev. John Gouldrick, C.M.; Rev. Patrick Griffin, C.M.; Rev. Stephen Grozio, C.M.; Rev. John Holliday, C.M.; Rev. John Kettelberger, C.M.; Rev. Jerry Luttenberger, C.M.; Rev. Timothy Lyons C.M.; Rev. James Maher, C.M.; Rev. John Maher, C.M.; Rev. Robert Maloney, C.M.; Rev. Tomaz Mavric, C.M.; Rev. Jack McKenna, C.M.; Rev. Tom McKenna C.M.; Sr. Patty Ann O'Brien, D.C.; Rev. Richie Rock, C.M.; Rev. Astor Rodriguez, C.M.; Rev. Aidan Rooney, C.M.; Sr. Louise Sullivan, D.C.; Rev. Jack Timlin, C.M.; Rev. Michael Whalen, C.M.; and many more.

To my Franciscan family, and the wonderful teachers and leaders at St. Francis Preparatory High School, especially Len Antinori; Sr. Diane Capuano OP; Bro. Leonard Conway, OFM; Dr. Patrick McLoughlin; Sr. Peggy McVetty, OP; Lorainne Smith; Rev. William Sweeney (LGM); among many others who left their mark on my soul.

To the many priests who reveal Christ's love, especially Rev. Gerard Sauer and Rev. Msgr. Robert Thelen for inviting me to serve in youth ministry; Rev. Francis Colamaria for your friendship and refreshments over the years, and Rev. Ignatius Catanello for your monthly inspiration over pea soup and grilled cheese.

To the spiritual and servant leaders, advocates, justice warriors, and ancient and contemporary prophets who fill these pages and form my conscience.

To the Diocese of Brooklyn, especially the Catholic Youth Ministry Initiative and the School of Evangelization for their support of youth and young adult formation.

To my friends in parish and youth ministry, especially Lucia Morales; Paul Morisi; Chris and Victoria Urena; Angela Marin; Frank and Cat Marin; Joe and Danielle Marin; Lauren and Robbie Pizzo; and all the young people we served and served with at the parish.

To my friends who share in this life's journey, especially Nicole and Chris Avery; Alison Behan; Giuliano Bruschi; Jeff Byrnes; Bethany Coston; Liz Coston; Paula DeBlasio;

Georgia and Jack DiSanto; Mike and Maryann Keighron; Amanda Kennedy; Bobby and Patrick Kiley-Rendon; Cheryl Llewelyn; Albert Santangelo; Fred Scholfield; Tom Seegel; Anne Thompson; Ralph "Coach" Wallace; and Carmelo, Vincenza, Rose, and Joseph Licata.

To my remarkable family, especially Dr. Raeann, Lt. Chris, my Godson A.J., Jamie, and Christopher Kyriakou; Cindy Holmes; and the Furimsky, Giove, Holmes, Hudlow, Kooy, Kuc, Kyriakou, Lund, Moran, Neglia, Sforza, Sikule, Sullivan, and Walters Families; among many others for your endless love and support.

To my wonderful parents Annette and Jim Walters for all of your love, sacrifices, and opportunity to become my true self. I am beyond blessed to call you my mom and dad.

To Dr. Suzie Walters for taking my hand and always believing in this dream, for rooting me in love and justice, and for making my life amazing.

To my Shea, thank you for inspiring me every day and revealing God's unconditional love. I love you to the moon and back.

To all the dreamers who change the world by knowing and reflecting God's love.

INTRODUCTION

Aren't you tired?

Isn't it exhausting, always settling instead of excelling?

Are you living your dream life, where you wake up most mornings excited for the day? Or, do you drag along, serving out a life-sentence in an unrewarding job, or in unappreciated relationships?

Do you feel disconnected from God, your life lacking inspiration and joy? Perhaps you even feel overwhelmed, burdened by life's pressures and obstacles.

There must be something more.

Looking within and looking out makes clear the many injustices of our divided society.

From the refugee searching for safety, to the adults and children forced into sexual slavery and labor, to the veterans living on the streets—cruelty haunts our human family.

You may feel anger, helplessness, numbness, grief.

Where is God?

At every moment God is trying to enter into our world and into your life. As with the disciples on Pentecost, who shared these same feelings and emotions, the Holy Spirit is moving, inviting you perhaps even charging you, to live a new life guided by Christ.

Still, each day—especially reading or watching the news, passing those hurting on the corner, feeling greatly for those wounded at your own table or in your own mirror—offers little comfort.

But comfort isn't the goal, nor is ignoring or accepting the distractions that pop up at every turn. Our emotions are speaking to us, calling us to respond. The Spirit is nudging us to, as the familiar saying states, "be the change we wish to see in the world." Transform your comfort into action. Turn to God to be that instrument of change. Change the world—starting with *your* world.

Now is the time to be that change, to be one with the Spirit. St Paul reminds us, "If we live by the Spirit, let us also be guided by the Spirit" (Gal 5:25). The Holy Spirit is inviting you to greater spiritual growth, to increased service and justice to those most in need, and to bring unity to a divided world.

+

You are meant to do more, to be your true self. Each day you are meant to wake up with a purpose, a purpose that God intended. You are meant to help solve the problems of this world. You are meant to live the life God intended when you were formed in your mother's womb.

This book can change your life. Just writing it has changed my life (I will explain more soon). These pages describe, as the title suggests, a dream—God's dream!

Your dreams can come true. Embrace them now, bring them into reality.

You are reading this book because a spiritual force is inviting you into your life's next chapter. Your rearview mirror reflects your life—its bumps and broken roads, as well as its sunny days and smooth paths.

Today and tomorrow offer opportunity. Every road, even a rocky one, can lead to a dream coming true.

Deep within I believe that God has a dream. God has over 7.4 billion dreams, instilled in every person living and breathing at this moment in history, in every day that came before and in every day yet to come.

God's dream includes you. Yes, You!

Can you, will you, believe this?

Now is the time to embrace God's dream for you.

That dream is deeply personal and also communal. God's dream is exclusively for you, but also that you bring justice and peace to those who need your voice, your ears, your talents, and your time.

+

In a world so divided, division seeming to grow by the day, look to Jesus just before he is arrested, tortured, then executed on the cross.

Jesus turns to his Father and offers a prayer that God be glorified, a prayer for His disciples, a prayer for every believer.

This is Jesus' prayer:

> *I ask not only on behalf of these, but also on behalf of those who will believe in me through their word, that they may all be one. As you, Father, are in me and I am in you, may they also be in us, so that the world may believe that you have sent me. The glory that you have given me I have given them, so that they may be one, as we are one, I in them and you in me, that they may become completely one, so that the world may know that you have sent me and have loved them even as you have loved me.* (Jn 17: 20-23)

This is Jesus' dream. It echoes down through the generations. Can we be the ones who finally let Jesus unite our divided world?

This rich prayer speaks to Jesus' desire that all his followers unite. Like a parent at the moment of death, he expresses his final wish just before his life will end. This is the mission of the Focolare Movement, an effort launched during a time of war and great suffering.

This desire for unity brings great hope—hope that by our unity, others will be attracted to Jesus, and to the unity of love. Tertullian noted what Romans said about the early Christians in Carthage: "see how they love one another."[1]

In this prayer, Jesus gives us the same glory that God gave Him. This glory is meant for us to change the world—to be one with God and to be one with one another. We are equipped with this glory by our very nature, a concept to be explored throughout this book.

Jesus' prayer is a love letter to God as much as it is a love letter to you. These pages will direct you to look within at your own gifts and to look without at the needs of the external world. May your life become a love letter back to God that shows how God's glory shines in you, and through you, in an effort of unity and love.

+

You are made in God's image. You, all your gifts, talents, joys, and yes, complexities, are of God.

An inventor creates an instrument to address a problem.

God, the greatest of inventors, made you—made each of us—to address the world's problems, the greatest being its lack of love.

You hold the power to bring your love, God's love, to another person, group, or situation.

But how?

Together, we can find the answer in your dreams.

These are not the dreams when you are sleeping, although those too can be helpful if you learn to remember and process them. Rather, it is the dreams of your heart that I invite you to discover.

But that invites another question: *what are your dreams?*

I am not talking about the superficial dreams, like perfect skin, or six pack abs, that society places on a pedestal and make you feel inferior when you don't measure up. I am not speaking of the size of your car, your home, or your savings account. I am speaking of your interior dreams, the ones at the core of your true identity as a reflection of Jesus.

These dreams, when you devote time and energy to them, make you feel excited and fill you with sudden joy.

These dreams keep you up at night, give you such a rush of energy that you can barely contain it, make you believe that all is possible.

These dreams guide you to become who you are meant to be, not just for you but for everyone else, too. By living your best life, using your God-given gifts, you will give love and model passion and that makes those around you better.

This book will guide you through a process, illustrated with lessons of spiritual teachers and life experiences, to recognize and live God's dream for you.

This process follows an organizational development model called Appreciative Inquiry. Although this model is typically used in corporations and in educational support services, this book applies it in guiding you to a more abundant life, a life that brings you joy, a life that brings joy to others in need.

Surely some aspects of your life are going well. Certain parts of your life may be filled with blessings, and you are using your gifts and talents in fruitful ways. Thank God for such blessings, and those who make them possible. You will be invited to increase these gifts and talents, to use them for God's glory.

Surely some aspects of your life are not fulfilling, or leave you yearning for more. Some situations that you see in the world and within your very self may require a new, creative response to uphold and affirm human dignity. You and your dreams can do that.

My writing this very book is one such example. After fifteen years of working with and supporting college-aged, junior high school, and high school students, I felt a calling to put pen to paper. I saw and continue to see so many young people (and people of all ages) chasing false dreams of fame and fortune rather than sharpening their God-given tools to help those most in need. The more division grows in the world, the greater the need to build unity. This book offers a strategy to do just that.

In the Gospel of John, Jesus asks His disciples, "'Do you also wish to go away?" (Jn 6:67). In asking this, Jesus seems heartbroken. His ministry and His purpose required his friends to accept this invitation of life of love, and he does not know if they will stay or if they will go.

Will they preach and live this gospel of love?

Will they heal the broken, bring together the divided, and love the unloved?

Today Jesus asks you this same question.

Will you leave too? Or will you stay?

Will you let Christ be your inner guide to true freedom and to unconditional love? Will you be the answer to someone's prayers?

Will you allow your dreams to come true?

+

This book is the result of one of my dreams. I always felt that I was meant to write it, but it wasn't easy. My journey took me down many broken roads. Through it all, I knew deep within that I was born to write. That sense did not always capture my attention and my time, but in the depth of my heart a steady, quiet voice was calling me, urging me, to write of God's love for us, and how we can express that love in many ways and vocations.

At a young age, I knew my vocations. A voice deep within called me to be a spouse, a father, a writer. At times, none of it seemed possible. Now, all have come about.

I felt a steady, sometimes nagging, yet empowering invitation from God telling me that this is what I was meant to do. I was created for this. And the universe provided nudges along the way.

Recently, as I was struggling to write an earlier version of this Introduction, I was feeling down. At a brewery in Brooklyn I saw a man wearing a t-shirt that said: "Write like you're running out of time." That message was random, but urgent. It was just the shove I needed to get back on course. Later that week, I came upon something that Dr. Martin Luther King Jr. said to junior high school graduates in Philadelphia in 1967: "When you discover what you are going to be in your life, set out to do it as if God Almighty called you at this particular moment in history to do it.[2]

+

While writing this book, I faced several social and personal challenges. They allowed me to discover my voice in a deeper way, one that I could not have anticipated or imagined. At one time I had found peace in being an empathetic listener, holding back in the gray of life. But personal, national, and global issues forced me to move from a comfortable middle to what was right. Family tragedy forced me to look deeply within and without, and so learn more about myself and more about God's unconditional mercy and love.

A random message, a personal tragedy can open for us a point of departure. We discover a road to something more.

Joseph Campbell writes:

> The adventure of the hero represents the moment in his life when he achieved illumination, the nuclear moment when, while still alive, he found and opened the road to the light beyond the dark walls of our living death.

You are called to be a hero, and so a hero for others. You set off on the road to the light by recognizing your dreams and accepting them as a mandate. At times you finally welcome these dreams because a crack opens up in your armor. At other times, you pursue your dreams because you are finally ready to be your true self. The dreams discussed here are not external, but internal. They are the dreams God has for you and for all of God's beautiful creation.

God does not dream that we succeed as society might suggest. God's dream is that we succeed in being our true self. God knows what we are made for; although we may not yet see the path for which we are made, it lies before us, waiting for us to see the light and pursue it.

+

This book provides strategies for envisioning your unique path. These pages help you recognize what you are truly called to be, what you are truly called to do for others.

Part I (chapters 1-3) identify who God is to you, and how God is calling you to bring to life God's dreams, found in the depth of your heart and soul. These three chapters will help you name who God is to you.

The rest of the book uses the wisdom and strategies of Appreciative Inquiry to outline clear and exciting steps to identifying and fulfilling God's dreams for you and for the world. The steps of Appreciative Inquiry include reflective activities to identify your gifts and talents, discover your dreams, and put them into action. This process makes up *Part II (chapters 4-6)*, *Part III (chapters 7-9)*, and *Part IV (chapters 10-11)*.

As you prepare to set off on this journey, it is critical to recognize a fundamental principle of this approach. That principle is love. And this love is God.

The core of who we are is love. Many faith traditions and spiritualities believe that we are made in the image and likeness of God. And God is love.

Our own life experiences provide insights into this love. They reveal God's unconditional and deep love for each and every person.

Consider moments when you felt an overwhelming sense of love for another. These moments provide glimpses of God's love for you, for each and every person.

It could be in a new relationship, where you can think only about that individual. It could be in a sacred ritual where you pledge yourself to that person. It could be after fifty years, when you watch that partner take his or her last breath.

It could be when a woman feels a child growing within her, or when a new baby holds your finger for that first time. It could be when you see your loved one truly happy, or when you can do nothing but simply be with loved ones as they mourn. God's love could be reflected in the encounter with a man living on the street, or a senior citizen sitting alone. It could be the moment when someone you love leaves or is taken away, or when you are struck by the pain of a person's poverty or illness.

Love captures all of this. It is what made Gandhi, in his desire for peace and justice, refuse to eat. It is what made Jesus cry when his friend Lazarus died. It is what brings us to sacrifice our own life, in small and big ways, for another person.

All such experiences let us see the love of our true self, a self that is divine. Recognizing that such love is courageous can change our life's narrative. Love reveals itself in many ways, but distractions constantly confront us, noises that prevent us from being free, from seeing the face of God within one another and within ourselves.

In *Here and Now* Henri Nouwen notes, "Spiritual reading is reading with an inner attentiveness to the movement of God's Spirit in our outer and inner lives. With that attentiveness, we will allow God to read us and to explain to us what we are truly about."[3]

Allow these pages to let God explain to you your very existence. Consider this book as a gift to discover what you are truly about, to discover God's dream for you. That is a dream for all of us in our universality and connectedness. And as I was reminded in Brooklyn by a t-shirt, we have no time to lose.

PART I

EMBRACING GOD'S DREAM

CHAPTER 1

APPRECIATING YOU & GOD

Every fall semester, I teach a first-year seminar course at St. John's University in Queens, New York. My initial lecture begins with the following question: "Why are you here?"

Every year the students are puzzled, and seek clarification by asking their own questions, such as:

- "Why are we here in class?"
- "Why are we here on earth at this time in human history?"
- "Why are we alive?"

The last clarifying question has the greatest implications.

"Why are we alive?"

It is a question that ancient philosophers wrestled with, that all religions attempt to answer. We all struggle with this one, yet how you answer drives all other questions and answers.

For eighteen-year-olds on their first day of college, such a question can be overwhelming. It is a question that we revisit throughout the semester as they are form their identity and future.

As challenging as the question is, the answer is quite simple.

The answer is to love God, ourselves, and others.

The Golden Rule

This love that guides us is formulated in the golden rule, true to all faith traditions. It is what Jesus responded with when asked about the greatest of the commandments (Mt 7:12). Greek philosopher Isocrates, over 300 years before Jesus lived, said "Do not do to others that which angers you when they do it to you."[4]

From the Hadith in the Islamic tradition, the prophet Muhammed said, "That which you want for yourself, seek for mankind That which you want for yourself, seek for mankind."[5]

Buddha, in the sixth century BCE, said, "Hurt not others in ways that you yourself would find hurtful."[6]

In Sikhism, the Golden Rule is similar: "Precious like jewels are the minds of all. To hurt them is not at all good. If thou desirest thy Beloved, then hurt thou not anyone's heart."[7]

The Tao Te Ching in the sixth century BCE, wrote, "The sage has no heart of his own, but takes the heart of the people as his heart."[8]

Similarly, Confucius said, "What you do not wish for yourself, do not do to others."[9]

Throughout history, we find the common thread of this similar rule or guide. No wonder it is known as the "golden" rule.

We are connected more than we can imagine. It is heartbreaking that wars are made in the name of religion when this commandment of love is at the core of who we are as people of faith.

We must start holding this rule as a sacred truth that can heal and unite our world.

Loving our God, ourselves, and one another is the answer to why we live. Throughout the centuries, and woven through our faith traditions, we find our purpose.

One of the key aspects of these teachings is to treat others as you would like to be treated. The danger in human nature is that those who hurt others are often hurting inside. Likely hurt by others in the past, there are many living an "un-golden" rule, hurting others as they have been hurt.

Some versions of the Golden Rule say to love as God loves you. The problem is that many feel unloved by God. They blame God, they feel hurt or betrayed by God. This is an understandable response, understood in psychology as a part of the grieving process. Unfortunately, many get "stuck" here.

Perhaps you feel this way now. If you do, God's dreams will likely be of no interest as your past experiences have been nightmares.

You are invited to understand God as the source of love. God is an ever-present, living source knocking at your heart. This chapter, and those that follow, focus on appreciating God as a source of unconditional love. Once you accept this, then even when hurt you can love. Then, despite your wounds and scars—and eventually in gratitude for them—you can love God back.

God's dream for you is love. Love in all its forms. Even when you feel unloved and alone, lost and confused, God is there. You may not see it or feel it, but that does not mean that God isn't loving you. You are invited to re-imagine who God is, and how God loves you.

This requires a connection to God. In this new awareness, you can see one another as a reflection of the same divine light that is central to our own identity. It starts with understanding who God is, then who we are as God's beloved, followed by our relationship with others because we are loved by God. This is the natural progression to living a life where your dreams, God's dreams, come true.

The road to discovering God's dreams is shaped by the Appreciative Inquiry model. The next part of this chapter explores the model in greater depth, including a brief exploration of your true and false self. This thread is woven throughout this book. The chapter concludes with a short reflection on your relationship with God and a model of prayer that can change the way you look at life.

Appreciating You: Background into Appreciative Inquiry

The journey that this book offers is greatly influenced by a process known as Appreciative Inquiry. The four steps of Appreciative Inquiry guide the later chapters of this book. This organizational model, developed by David Cooperrider, focuses on the positive within a person, or an organization.[10] Instead of asking what the problem is, or what is not working, the questions focus instead on what is successful, and what is working.

This book uses Appreciative Inquiry's steps to help you appreciate your past, find gratitude in the present, and achieve your dreams for the future.

- The Discover step inspires Chapters 4-6.
- The Dream step inspires chapters 7-9
- The Design and Deliver steps inspire chapter 10-11.

I work intimately with Appreciative Inquiry and a similar model, Appreciative Advising, geared toward education. I apply Appreciative Inquiry to my ministry with young people, ages twelve to twenty-three. I also use it as a consultation tool for youth ministers, campus ministers, and in both the first-year seminar and doctoral courses that I instruct. Appreciative Inquiry was also utilized in establishing Catholic Scholars, an award-winning faith-based leadership program at St. John's University.

I am excited to share these principles, activities, and inspiration with you as you begin to appreciate what is already working within you, and then moving you to a place of living the best life that God wants and needs you to live.

Your True Self

By the time you complete this book, you will clearly identify your dreams and an appropriate action plan to bring them to life. Supporting this process will be lessons from spiritual leaders and scripture, and real-life examples to help guide you.

One of the key themes to be explored is this idea of your True Self.

As you begin to explore your dreams, you will distinguish between dreams that are of and for God, and dreams that are feeding your ego, or that superficial part of yourself that meets your external, societal needs.

A great deal of work in the history of spirituality and human consciousness focuses on the idea of True Self. Consider these words from Marcus Tullius Cicero (b.106 BCE), the famous Roman orator and philosopher: "For that man whom your outward form reveals are not yourself; the spirit is the true self, not that physical figure which can be pointed out by your finger."[11]

The golden rule explored earlier speaks to this inner light that is divine. In the Judeo-Christian tradition, this concept of True Self begins in how we were created—in the image of God (see Gen 1:26-27).

Fr. Richard Rohr writes:

> You (and every other created thing) begin with your unique DNA, an inner destiny as it were, an absolute core that knows the truth about you, a true believer tucked away in a cellar of your being, an imago Dei that begs to be allowed, to be fulfilled, and to show itself "You were chosen in Christ

before the world was made—to stand before God in love—marked out beforehand
as fully adopted sons and daughters" (Eph
1:4-5). This is your True Self. Historically,
it was often called the "soul."[12]

The True Self speaks to the soul, but the False Self
speaks to an external illusion.

Thomas Merton explains the False Self:

Every one of us is shadowed by an illuso-
ry person: a false self. This is the man (or
woman) that I want myself to be but who
cannot exist, because God does not know
anything about him (or her).[13]

He adds:

My false and private self is the one who
wants to exist outside the reach of God's
will and God's love—outside of reality and
outside of life. And such a self cannot help
but be an illusion.

Merton writes often of True Self and False Self. In *And
Now I See...: A Theology of Transformation*, Bishop Robert
Barron offers this reflection on Merton:

For him, the spiritual life could be defined
as the awakening of the true "I," the Christ
living in me, and the dying to the vaporous
and destructive ego created by fear . . . It is
the struggle between two selves.[14]

In chapters 4-6, your true self will begin to be revealed
in the Discovery activities. You will begin to identify your
gifts and talents, and your joys.

Dream activities will follow, allowing God to speak to
and through you. The constant inner work of distinguish-

ing between what is of soul and of what is of ego is a life-long process. You need to reflect honestly and prayerfully as you journey through these Appreciative Inquiry steps to capture fully and truly the Christ living within you.

Barron uses the word "fear" in describing Merton's battle between the True and False Self. There is a certain amount of fear in our need for security, our need to belong, and our self-image. This is all at risk when we embrace our True Self. There is an even greater fear, the fear of truly believing in your divine light.

Please do not misinterpret this as a heretical statement. We are not God, and we are not the Savior who walked the earth 2,000 years ago. What we are is made in the image and likeness of God. God's divine light shines within me and within you. Can you, will you, believe this?

Can you, will you, not be afraid of this reality?

The poet Marianne Williamson famously writes, "Our deepest fear is that we are powerful beyond measure."[15] This power comes from God.

It is such divine power that lies at the core of this beautiful prayer of St. Teresa of Avila:

> *Christ has no body on earth but yours.*
>
> *No hand but yours.*
>
> *No feet but yours.*
>
> *Yours are the eyes through which Christ's*
>
> *Compassion for the world is to look out.*
>
> *Yours are the feet with which*
>
> *He is to go about doing good;*
>
> *And yours are the hand with*
>
> *Which He is to bless us now.*

If we truly come to believe these words, we must come to appreciate who God is and how God lives within us. This next part will explore this very concept and its potential impact.

Appreciating God

As children, we learned that God is in heaven. Television and film depict this scene in similar ways, typically as an older white male with a long beard standing among the clouds. The inspiration comes from medieval art that attempted to capture the majesty of heaven and its king. These images reflect the patriarchal and European influences upon the artists, and the patrons who supported them.

Although we live in a scientific age where we can even see what the earth looks like from outer space, we still hold with conventional images. Even the Bible depicts heaven as a grand feast or celebration.

Metaphors are important, as they relate to our lived experiences. They are also dangerous as they can limit, or even misdirect, our understanding (or sense of understanding) of who God is, and what returning to this Source involves.

The names we give to the divine—God, Jesus, Source, Spirit—cannot capture the essence of our Creator. But once in sacred scriptures God's identity is revealed. In the book of Exodus, the Spirit of God speaks to Moses in a burning bush. Moses asks, "If I come to the Israelites and say to them, 'The God of your ancestors has sent me to you,' and they ask me, 'What is his name? What shall I say to them? God said to Moses, 'I am who I am.' He said further, 'Thus you shall say to the Israelites, "I am has sent me to you"'" (Ex 3:13-14).

Wayne Dyer, a spiritual teacher I esteem greatly and who I reference frequently in this book, wrote and spoke of this identification. He notes how we often begin a sentence with "I am," but then follow it with a negative word. Because we do not recognize our own divinity and awesomeness, we limit ourselves.

Dyer writes, "The words 'I am,' which you consistently use to define who you are and what you are capable of, are holy expressions for the name of God—the highest aspect of yourself."[16]

Consider how often you say negative ideas about yourself.

"I am not good enough."

"I am not skinny enough."

"I am not smart enough."

I could go on and on.

Dyer notes what we are really saying. Because of our own divinity, in such statements we can interchange "I am" with "God is."

So, when you are making negative statements, you are really saying:

"God is not good enough."

"God is not skinny enough."

"God is not smart enough."

This cannot be true. It is untrue when you say it about God, and it is untrue when you say it about yourself.

When you speak like this, you fail to recognize your own divinity. Sure, God is in heaven, wherever heaven is. But God is also within you, and in all things. The core of Ignatian spirituality focuses on "finding God in all things." This search also includes finding God within you.

Consider these words from ancient Hindu scriptures:

The human body is the temple of God.

One who kindles the light of awareness within gets true light.

The sacred flame of your inner shrine is constantly bright.

The experience of unity is the fulfillment of human endeavors.

The mysteries of life are revealed.[17]

You are invited to recognize God, the sacred flame of your inner shrine. Sometimes such recognition comes through grand, memorable, spiritual experiences. But it also comes through daily reflection on the search for God within you, and within all who you encounter.

The Examen

The Ignatian tradition offers a helpful spiritual practice known as *the Examen,* created by St. Ignatius Loyola, a Spanish priest from the sixteenth century. He founded the Society of Jesus, the Jesuits, known today for their impact on education, specifically higher education. Loyola contributed spiritual practices and meditations, the most popular being the Examen.

The Examen offers a process that Jim Manney explains in *A Simple Life-Changing Prayer*:

"The Examen is a method of reviewing your day in the presence of God. It's actually an attitude more than a method, a time set aside for thankful reflection on where God is in your everyday life."[18] It includes five steps that take less than twenty minutes to complete. Here are the steps with a short prayer that Manney offers:

1. **Ask God for Light**: I want to look at my day with God's eyes, not merely my own.

2. **Give Thanks**: The day I have just lived is a gift from God. Be grateful for it.

3. **Review the Day**: I carefully look back on the day just completed, being guided by the Holy Spirit.

4. **Face your Shortcomings**: I face up to what is wrong—in my life and in me.

5. **Look toward the day to come**: I ask where I
   need God in the day to come.

This method begins to reshape your attitude throughout the day. You can look at life differently.

The first step recognizes the divinity within and before
you. Another way to say this is, "God, allow me to see the
light within me and within others." I will speak more to
this concept later.

The second step is one of gratitude. All spiritual practices emphasize this need to say "thank you" to our source
for the blessings of life. In the opening scene of the spiritual film, *The Shift*, in the early morning Wayne Dyer emerg-
es from his bed saying, "thank you, thank you, and thank
you." It is a powerful scene that I try to implement each
morning.

The third step is an opportunity to reflect on all your
daily interactions and experiences. As I was writing this
book, I was struck by something Fr James Martin, SJ, said
about the Examen in his weekly podcast.

The words were: "pay attention."

He invited listeners to "pay attention" to how God is
speaking to us in our daily interactions. I find that when I
pay attention, God responds. Despite my ego's resistance, I
receive the gift of clarity and understanding.

This notion of paying attention brings to mind a scriptural quote, "Do not neglect to show hospitality to strangers, for by doing that some have entertained angels without
knowing it" (Heb 13:2). In a similar way, in the poem "The
Guest House," Rumi says, "Be grateful for whoever comes,
because each has been sent as a guide from beyond."[19]

When you take time to reflect, especially with this
mindset, you will begin to look at life differently. Maybe
the inconsiderate people in line at the grocery store or in
the car next to you can be viewed differently when you reflect on what they may have been going through in that

moment. By reflecting, we see life and its daily interactions as constant encounters with angels, or even more appropriate, with God.

The fourth step presents an opportunity to address your shortcomings. At the end of your day, revisit your thoughts and decisions that need to be recognized and reconciled.

These uncomfortable insights are never easy, but they do allow for you to learn and grow.

Reflecting on my day (or my life) lets surface my potential to be a great teacher. The lesson I often learn is one of freedom. I am called to allow others to be free. I am called to free myself from controlling how people feel or act. When I use spiritual vision, I see my shortcomings as opportunities to move into a higher spiritual level. These are my daily tests, and my desire to fix things is one of the greatest.

You can also recognize your shortcomings while reflecting on your day and your encounters by asking yourself this question: "What annoys you?" Carl Jung wrote, "Everything that irritates us about others can lead us to a better understanding of ourselves."[20]

This reflective process presents an opportunity to learn and grow from your interactions with others, even the difficult ones.

The fifth and final step of the Examen is to look to tomorrow, asking where you need God. This helps you prepare for the following day. Surrendering to the Source will leave you vulnerable, but it changes your attitude and the way you experience life. I encourage you to include the prayer, "God, allow me to bring your light to those who need it tomorrow." This continues to envision the next day as an encounter with the divine. This spiritual exercise is just one method to change our approach to life in the search for God.

However you pray, just pray! Be in relationship with God.

"Praying is living," says Henri Nouwen. "It is eating and drinking, action and rest, teaching and learning, playing and working. Praying pervades every aspect of our lives. It is the unceasing recognition that God is wherever we are, always inviting us to come closer and to celebrate the divine gift of being alive."[21]

Closing Thoughts

This chapter invited you to gain a greater appreciation for yourself and for the key role that God plays in your life. Understanding this allows for an inspiring and united approach to living a life of love.

The Appreciative Inquiry steps of Discover, Dream, Design, and Deliver guide your dreams and allow you to take significant steps in your search for love and joy.

It is difficult to understand yourself as created by God and own your own divinity. So often you place God at a distance, an imaginary force in the clouds or an inaccessible statue on a pedestal. God is so much more. Changing the way you pray through an approach like the Examen will begin to shift your perceptions. You will see an intimate God who lives within you and within others.

This shift requires trust. *Do you trust God?*

And do you trust that God has a dream for you?

Exploring this requires asking yourself, Is there a God? If you answer yes to that question, the next is: Do you believe God cares about you?

You can add: Do you believe God has dreams for you?

Answering this may be really difficult. Even a yes may come with understandable hesitancy. The difficultly in answering depends upon how you see God. More accurately, it depends upon how you were taught to see God. Life's difficulties may also add to your mistrust or hesitancy.

The next chapter invites you into a different understanding of who God is, supported by events in my own
life that allowed me to come to know, trust, and love God.
This insight will invite you to trust me, coming to know
one example of why I believe in God's dreams for all of
creation, especially in you.

CHAPTER 2

BLIND LOVE

To understand God's dream for you, you must come to understand God's inherent role in your life.

Take a moment to consider how St. Josephine Bakhita saw God:

> Seeing the sun, the moon and the stars, I said to myself, "Who could be the Master of these beautiful things?" I felt a great desire to see Him, to know Him, and to pay Him homage.[22]

Would you say the same as this former slave who faced horrendous torture and abuse?

Who is God to you?

The last chapter invited you to see God as "I Am," reminding you of this intimate relationship. The second part of the chapter provided a tool to pray differently, reflecting on each day as an internal and external encounter with God.

This chapter focuses on God's unconditional love, despite the worst of humanity, and what needs the most work within.

The misconception of God as judge and jury creates a fear that can separate us from our creator. This "reward and punishment" relationship is an immature understanding of God. Later in this chapter, through one of

Jesus' most popular parables, you will come to see God as God truly is.

First, let me share how I came to this understanding—as the result of a constant urging of the Universe. Dyer called them "spiritual breadcrumbs." I call them heavenly nudges.

Psychology and spirituality speak of "synchronicity," a concept first introduced by Jung but reinforced and explored in spiritual writings and circles. Jung described synchronicity as "events that are 'meaningful coincidences' if they occur with no causal relationship yet seem to be meaningfully related."[23]

My greatest experience of this occurred when I was twenty-one. I was a senior at St. John's University, and over the course of five months, it seemed that everywhere I turned I encountered Rembrandt's *Return of the Prodigal Son*. This chapter begins with an account of this encounter, which changed my life. Afterwards, I explore more deeply the story of the Prodigal Son and a book related to the painting.

In sharing this experience, I pray you will not only come to see God's unconditional love, but also the movement of the Holy Spirit that is calling you into a deeper authentic relationship with God.

A Book and the Parable

This experience of synchronicity started with Art and Christianity, a course in the final semester of my undergraduate studies. The main text was *The Return of the Prodigal Son* by Henri Nouwen, who became one of my favorite spiritual authors. Nouwen was a Catholic priest whose greatest conversion moment came while serving in a community for the severely disabled, L'Arche Daybreak, near Toronto, Canada.

Nouwen writes of a pastoral ministry focused on the encounter—an opportunity to be transformed and inspired. In *The Return of the Prodigal Son,* Nouwen speaks of his own synchronicity with the painting of the same name, created by the seventeenth-century Dutch artist Rembrandt.[24] Nouwen examines the portrait of a forgiving father and his lost sons, based on the Gospel of Luke parable.

In this famous parable (Lk 15:11-32) Jesus explains that the younger son asks for his inheritance, which would be the same as asking for his father to be dead. That son then spends all this money, only to face starvation during a great famine. He returns to his father, not to seek reconciliation, as he did not expect one, but to survive by working for his father.

Overwhelmed with joy, the father runs to his son. He tells the servants to kill the fatted calf as there will be a celebration. His son receives a ring, new clothes, and is welcomed home with open arms.

Later that night, returning from work, the older son sees that there is a party. Finding out that his younger brother has returned, he is furious. He had been faithful to his father, working hard on the land, only to see his brother welcomed after squandering his inheritance.

The older son presses the father, and here the father provides a famous line from scripture, ". . . but we had to celebrate and rejoice, because this brother of yours was dead and has come to life; he was lost and has been found" (Lk 15:32).

Rembrandt depicts the father and son as looking similar. They dress in the same robes and have long beards. However, Nouwen and art historians point out some important differences.

The father's hands are open, whereas the older brother's hands are closed. The father embraces the son who is kneeling before him. He is offering himself in love. The father's eyes also appear to be blind. He sees the son not with human eyes, but divine.

Jesus is asking us to do the same in our relationships with one another. He is revealing how God loves us.

I recall hearing this parable as a child in church. I picture it as if it were yesterday. I was sitting in the same pew where my family sat each Sunday, near the middle and to the far left. The priest read the parable, and I thought, "The older son should be mad. It isn't fair." Even at a young age, this lesson challenged me.

It is even more difficult because it involves family. For better and for worse, with family we feel things differently. This is why in many families some relatives do not speak and need reconciliation. Some issues are recent; some go back decades, even to childhood. How many reconciliations did not occur until the funeral of a loved one? How many waited too long, leaving the living with regret instead of peace?

This is one of the key messages of this parable. What matters is that the son is alive. God desires the unity of relationships for God's children. Offering forgiveness can be more of a gift to yourself than it is to the other person.

The father in this parable demonstrates the mercy that God always offers. God's love is unconditional, limitless, not bound to anyone or anything. All we have to do is return to our God where we will find God waiting for us, happy that we are home.

The Painting and a Bishop

My first encounter with Rembrandt's painting was the cover of Nouwen's book, but it would not be my last. As I was reading the book, I went on a senior retreat. Although I had been closely involved in service and ministry, this was the only retreat I attended as a university student. When I arrived that first night, I was awe-struck to discover that the theme was "Coming Home." In the middle of the main room, surrounded by candles, was a framed print of Rembrandt's painting.

At first, I thought it was a coincidence. Throughout the retreat, I recognized that this was no coincidence at all. God was inviting me to see life, and God, in a deeper, more meaningful way.

The painting continued to appear. Several weeks later, I went into Student Life to drop off paperwork, only to find a poster of this painting on an office door. Later that week, in my parents' mail was a magazine with—guess what—a cover that included Rembrandt's painting. God was clearly trying to teach me something. This was a consistent heavenly nudge inviting me into exploration and love.

I believe this painting helped prepare me for a life in ministry, and after years of reflection, it also reinforced what I was taught by the Franciscan, Vincentian, and Marist communities in my Catholic formation and education.

During this senior year, and for several years after, I would have a monthly lunch at a local diner with a great spiritual advisor, Ignatius Catanello (better known to many as Iggy). He was a parish priest, an auxiliary bishop in the Diocese of Brooklyn, and a professor at St. John's. We met through a mutual friend who at a very young age had passed away from lymphoma. At our monthly lunches, Iggy would model living in spirit. He was as great of a listener as he was a teacher. One of his favorite lines, "as the great saints teach us…," was always followed by a simple but profound lesson from a saint or saints.

After one lunch, spring was in the air and we took the opportunity to walk back to his church. He invited me into his living area, and there, centered on his wall, was a framed replica of *The Return of the Prodigal Son*. I started to tell him about how this painting continued to appear in my life. He explained that he brought it back from Rome, and the important lessons it reveals about God's love.

A month later, I received a call from the rectory. Iggy's secretary told me that the bishop left a graduation gift for me at the office. I stopped by after my last class, and she handed me a large package. I took it to the car, and once inside, unwrapped it. I was moved to tears. It was the framed print I had seen on his wall. I immediately called him to say thank you, and to also say that I could not possibly accept it (I couldn't imagine how difficult it must have been for him to carry this framed print on a plane and through customs).

He said, "This painting belongs to you." He added, "Someone will give me something else to put on the wall." The next time I visited, sure enough, there was another spiritual image in its place.

As I moved into ministry the following year, that painting found a place on my office wall, and wherever I have moved, Iggy's painting is dead center. It will always be there until someone else can benefit from this image. In my years of ministry, I have used the painting countless times with students to demonstrate God's love, and the call for us to love in the same way. It is a gift that keeps on giving. I recall meeting with college students amidst broken relationships, broken hearts, and broken spirits. I recall students who were hurt and misused, while others were searching, and confused. Iggy's generosity served, and continues to serve, as a model of God's love for me and for my students.

I remember one student who saw God as strict and vengeful. His biological father provided as much of this inspiration as some of the more striking depictions in the Old Testament. I pointed to Rembrandt's painting, specifically the hands of the father. Earlier, I described how his hands were open, unlike the older son's. Another interesting detail is that one hand is depicted as more muscular, while the other smaller and more feminine. Art historians believe this signifies the paternal and maternal love of God. This student had never imagined God as maternal. Thankfully, his mother was kind to him, and he was able to see God more clearly as he related his experience with his mother's love. This painting allowed the student to see God's love.

Nine years after I received this gift, after a lengthy illness, Iggy passed away. At his wake, I learned two final lessons from him.

First, was the simplicity of his coffin, a basic wooden box. Unlike most coffins I had seen at wakes and funerals, it was thin and fragile. During the funeral, it was explained that as a Third Order Franciscan, Iggy had taken a vow of simplicity. It all made sense now. This is why he could so easily give away a framed painting that hung at the center of his wall. Like St. Francis, he was not attached to anything. He simply lived to serve.

The second thing I noticed was the extremely large crowd. Sure, there were other bishops, priests, and vowed religious brothers and sisters. But there were many people like me, and of all ages. They were there because in some small way, he made them feel special. At the wake, I was surprised to see a friend and classmate with her father and family. She explained how Iggy was an important influence for her father. Sitting in the pews at the wake, he shared, "Iggy reached out to guys like me, the guys who didn't always go to church." He added, "He just wanted us to know that God loves us. He helped me through some difficult times."

I heard similar stories over those days. Iggy walked with people on the journey, often over a bowl of pea soup at the local diner or an espresso at an Italian cafe. He was like the father in the painting and in the parable. When you were with him, he was simply happy you were there, and we in turn, were happy to be with him. Like Nouwen said at the start of this chapter, Iggy "chose to share our pain and touch our wounds with a warm and tender hand."

Every time I left his company, he would say something about how special I was, not only to the university where I worked, or the students I ministered to, but also to him. It was his way of making me, and all he broke bread with at this corner diner, know that we were loved. Not just by him, but by God.

As I understand God's love, I find that it is blind. We may think we are right in our judgments of others and of ourselves, but God calls us into something deeper. We are called to embrace one another with unconditional love. Just as God loves us, we are called to love one another.

Even after all these years, this parable continues to speak to me, reminding me of Iggy, and of God's unconditional love. This occurs most often at St. Thomas More Church on the Queens campus of St. John's University.

One of the main stained-glass windows depicts the parable. At the start and at the end of the academic year (September and April), the sun can make the window almost impossible to see. Where I normally sit and stand, the light shines so strongly through the glass it can temporarily blind me.

It is the perfect reminder of God's blind and unconditional love given to me and to you. When you are blind as Rembrandt's father is depicted, you can love blindly. As Meister Eckhart says, "The eye with which I see God is the same one with which God sees me. My eye and God's eye is one eye, and one sight, and one knowledge, and one love."[25]

Closing Thoughts

This chapter invites you to see your creator as one who loves you unconditionally, who is constantly trying to reach you. This is an invitation to a life of greater love and greater joy.

The Holy Spirit reveals this love in art and books, in teachers and mentors, in loved ones, and in strangers. There is no limit to God's love, and to how God reminds you of this love for you. You simply need to open your eyes and your heart to see the father running toward you with open arms because you are God's beloved.

The next chapter focuses on a key question of this book: What is God's dream?

Soon, you will be invited to discover your own dreams inspired by God, dreams that are unique to you. As they can change your life, they can also change the lives of those most in need.

With a greater understanding of God's love for you and for humanity, let's explore the dreams of our compassionate God.

CHAPTER 3

GOD'S DREAM

When you look with new eyes that focus on the divine your life takes a different approach. Your dreams also begin to take a different shape. In the next chapter, you will focus on discovering your unique gifts and talents, understanding in greater detail how the divine lives within you. In future chapters you will be invited to look inward, followed by the invitation to dream of your future in a new, inspired way. Before we do this, let's first gain insight into God's dream for you and for others.

To begin we will attempt to grasp what happens after we die (trusting there is an afterlife). No one knows for sure what to expect. I am not going to speculate on what exactly awaits you, but I can focus on one metaphor for heaven: God's kingdom.

God's Kingdom

Sacred scripture uses "kingdom" to explain what occurs after death. Envisioning kingdom as a place or destination connects with the image of God as "king." Like the metaphor of a great banquet or heavenly feast, this imagery speaks to power, structure, and reign.

In Christian scriptures, however, Jesus presents the notion of kingdom in a different way. He speaks of it not as a place or a destination, but as a present reality.

In the first chapter of the Gospel of Mark, Jesus "came to Galilee, proclaiming the good news of God, and saying,

'The time is fulfilled, and the kingdom of God is at hand. Repent, and believe in the good news.'" (Mk 1:14-15)

In his presentation on "Welcoming the Stranger," Rev. Bryan N. Massingale draws our attention to the word "repent," especially the original Greek term, "metanoia." This word does not mean just a change, but as Massingale explains, "a decisive break from how one has lived before to embrace the new life that Jesus offers, a life according to God's dream/vision of humankind."[26]

Jim Wallis explains this notion further, "Repentance is not just about being sorry or just feeling guilty. It is about turning in a new direction. The biblical word for repentance in the original Greek is metanoia, which means you are going in the wrong direction, and it's time to turn right around."[27]

Jesus presents the good news as a message of love. As discussed earlier, when challenged to identify the greatest of commandments, he offers the Golden Rule. It is a universal message that transcends generations and time, a message that those operating at the highest spiritual levels know and teach as truth. This love of self, of God, and of neighbor is the most important of life's lessons and directions. Only when you begin to understand the challenges and implications of living such a life can you repent and turn things around. This takes us on a journey of unconditional love for all.

In the Gospel of Matthew Jesus offers this roadmap:

> When the Son of Man comes in his glory, and all the angels with him, then he will sit on the throne of his glory. All the nations will be gathered before him, and he will separate people one from another as a shepherd separates the sheep from the goats, and he will put the sheep at his right hand and the goats at the left. Then the king will say to those at his right hand, "Come, you that are

blessed by my Father, inherit the kingdom
prepared for you from the foundation of the
world; for I was hungry and you gave me
food, I was thirsty and you gave me something to drink, I was a stranger and you welcomed me, I was naked and you gave me
clothing, I was sick and you took care of me,
I was in prison and you visited me." Then
the righteous will answer him, "Lord, when
was it that we saw you hungry and gave you
food, or thirsty and gave you something to
drink? And when was it that we saw you a
stranger and welcomed you, or naked and
gave you clothing? And when was it that we
saw you sick or in prison and visited you?"
And the king will answer them, "Truly I tell
you, just as you did it to one of the least of
these who are members of my family, you
did it to me." Then he will say to those at
his left hand, "You that are accursed, depart
from me into the eternal fire prepared for
the devil and his angels; for I was hungry and
you gave me no food, I was thirsty and you
gave me nothing to drink, I was a stranger
and you did not welcome me, naked and you
did not give me clothing, sick and in prison
and you did not visit me." Then they also
will answer, "Lord, when was it that we saw
you hungry or thirsty or a stranger or naked
or sick or in prison, and did not take care of
you?" Then he will answer them, "Truly I
tell you, just as you did not do it to one of
the least of these, you did not do it to me."
(Mt 25: 31-46)

Jesus explains that the good news of the kingdom ar-
rives when we treat our brothers and sisters as we would

treat God. I find that God isn't always easy to relate to, as we are conditioned to treat God as a distant figure, or we lack an intimate relationship because we do not see God as a part of our humanity, and we do not see ourselves as a part of God's divinity.

When I speak to my students about encountering God in those they serve on the margins, I invite them to see in the poor their loved ones. When they bring sandwiches and clothes to the many individuals who call the streets of Manhattan home, I challenge them to see that person in need as their parent or grandparent. I ask them to feel for the stranger what they feel for those who they love the most.

This is what God requires of us. It is not a suggestion, but a mandate. This is how you are asked to love. You are asked to love when it is most difficult, when it is most uncomfortable. This is the journey to the kingdom.

As this section concludes, let's turn to Henri Nouwen once again, with his vision for a "peaceable kingdom:"

> The marvelous vision of the peaceable kingdom, in which all violence has been overcome and all men, women, and children live in loving unity with nature, calls for its realization in our day-to-day lives. Instead of being an escapist dream, it challenges us to anticipate what it promises. Every time we forgive our neighbor, every time we make a child smile, every time we show compassion to a suffering person, every time we arrange a bouquet of flowers, offer care to tame or wild animals, prevent pollution, create beauty in our homes and gardens, and work for peace and justice among peoples and nations we are making the vision come true.[28]

A Soul Named Francis

A powerful example of fulfilling this vision is an interaction between Francis of Assisi and a leper. Twentieth-century writer G.K. Chesterton described Francis as "a lover of God, and he really was a lover of men."[29] This was not always the case.

Lepers frightened Francis, which was understandable given the contagious nature of their disease. Jesus invited Francis to turn his life around by loving the least of his brothers and sisters.

In this decision Francis experienced conversion. Here is one of his conversion moments as told by one of his companions:

> One day while Francis was praying fervently to God, he received an answer: "O Francis, if you want to know my will, you must hate and despise all that which hitherto your body has loved and desired to possess. Once you begin to do this, all that formerly seemed sweet and pleasant to you will become bitter and unbearable, and instead, the things that formerly made you shudder will bring you great sweetness and content." Francis was divinely comforted and greatly encouraged by these words. Then one day, as he was riding near Assisi, he met a leper. He had always felt an overpowering horror of these sufferers, but making a great effort, he conquered his aversion, dismounted, and, in giving the leper a coin, kissed his hand. The leper then gave him the kiss of peace, after which Francis remounted his horse and rode on his way. Some days later he took a large sum of money to the leper hospital, and gathering all the inmates together, he gave them alms, kissing each of their hands.

> Formerly, he could neither touch or even look at lepers, but when he left them on that day, what had been so repugnant to him had really and truly been turned into something pleasant. Indeed, his previous aversion to lepers had been so strong, that, besides being incapable of looking at them, he would not even approach the places where they lived. And if by chance he happened to pass anywhere near their dwellings or to see one of the lepers, even though he was moved to give them alms through some intermediate person, he would nevertheless turn his face away and hold his nose. But, strengthened by God's grace, he was enabled to obey the command and to love what he had hated.[30]

Conversion moments to love what we hate, or what we do not understand, are not limited to great saints and spiritual leaders. We have conversion moments too, but at times we fail to recognize the change occurring within. The spiritual leaders that we uphold as saints and prophets teach us to pay attention to the conversion of our hearts. Sometimes, as for St. Vincent de Paul, only when he looked back at his life could he see God's hand moving through him in his interactions with others, especially those most in need. Reflecting on our daily life, as well as our past journey, lets us see how God is calling us to respond to the needs of this world. Later in this book you will be invited to reflect on your life journey to see how this is true for you.

When we look at the saints, before their conversion moments their lives were going in one direction, typically ordinary. Then, after an experience, often an uncomfortable or difficult situation, their life is never the same. For Francis of Assisi, in listening to Christ and in embracing the leper, his life became extraordinary—so extraordinary that some five hundred years after he took his last breath his life still speaks to us.

One of the most beloved spiritual figures in human history was once repulsed by his fellow man. Francis was moved, or as it was described, "strengthened by God's grace," to "obey the command to love what he had hated."[31] The command to love goes beyond loving those who love you back. It requires loving what makes you uncomfortable, repulsed, fearful. Massingale notes that "once you truly love your neighbor, or live with and for the stranger, you begin to be treated as the stranger. It becomes your cross to bear."[32]

The Burden of Leadership

Once revered in his community for his playful nature and family name, Francis became repulsive to others because of his simple lifestyle and his contact with lepers. People believed he was insane.

Dorothy Day, one of the great leaders and advocates for the poor in twentieth-century New York, was criticized immensely by people of her own religion, including its leaders, for her radical hospitality and love of the poor.

Jesus was mocked, ridiculed, and killed because of his gospel of love.

Because love is easily misunderstood it is often met with hate and fear. As connected as the developed world has become through the gift of technology, we are as divided as ever due to politics, religion, and the many "isms" of our time.

For example, consider faithful Muslims whose distinctive dress distinguishes them and so may be met with glances of skepticism, passing hateful comments, and in some cases, violent assaults—because of how they worship, live their lives, and come to know and worship God.

One recent example in my community happened in 2015, in Ozone Park, Queens. A fifty-five-year old Imam, Maulama Akonjee, and fellow cleric sixty-four-year old

Tharam Uddin, were killed after leaving afternoon prayers. In my younger years I walked these same blocks on the way to my church a short distance away.

Too often we hear of violence to religious leaders and worshipers alike. Mosques being threatened, temples with extra police presence, and churches riddled with gunfire. In a place of heavenly peace, violence often follows. And it is the religious leaders who often take the fall.

In 1995, Israeli Prime Minister Yitzhak Rabin was assassinated because of his peace initiatives (and potential forfeiting of occupied territories). A year earlier, along with Yasser Arafat and Shimon Peres, he was awarded the Nobel Peace Prize for fashioning the Oslo Accords. Some considered this to be a great movement in peace. Despite his critical work and international recognition, some considered Rabin a traitor.

John Oswald Sanders, General Director of the Overseas Missionary Fellowship in the 1950s and 1960s reflected, "Often a crowd does not recognize a leader until he has gone, and then they build a monument to him with the stones they threw at him in life."[33]

So why take the risk? Why love in a way that is so extreme, and polarizing? Why invite violence, anger, misunderstanding?

We love because God loves. It is God's dream.

Love is the path to true peace.

Isn't love your true identity? Isn't it at your core?

This book started with a different question: "Aren't you tired?" If you answered yes, the remedy is to give—and receive—more love. When we operate out of love, we live a different life.

Take this common scenario as an example. Walking down the street you meet a stranger. The weather is cold and wet, and this person is not properly dressed for such conditions. Their clothes are dirty, as is their skin and hair. They may have a piece of cardboard explaining their life and their needs, or a cup filled with a few coins. They look at you, and they ask for food or for money. You have a choice. Do you stop and engage? Do you drop a dollar and keep walking? Do you avoid eye contact, pretend not to see the person, or talk on your phone to avoid communication? Do you say a silent prayer as you feel for their pain? Do you say a prayer for yourself as you walk away knowing you could do more, that you should do more? What do you do? What can you do?

In overcrowded New York City, this can be a daily experience. Those who live on the street seem to increase by the year, an observation confirmed by the Department of Homeless Services, whose recent research reveals more living on the streets than ever before. Not since the Great Depression has the problem been so severe for families with children. There are plenty of reasons—addictions, mental health issues, improper care for veterans and the elderly, difficult choices, the economy.

These realities scream for a response. And this is only one population in need. Countless other groups and individuals across the world need help desperately. Your dreams, from God, can and must provide at least a partial response to the cries of those most in need. You will explore this in greater detail later in the book, as you identify your dreams and bring them to life.

Our experience during these encounters with the stranger in our midst touches our humanity. It reveals something about us—it reveals our truth. It reveals our divinity. I have come to believe that our guilt when we do not engage with the stranger is healthy. It is a tug at our heart from our true, divine self to be and do better. It is a reminder to encounter the divine in the other, especially the lepers of our time.

Inspiration from a King

I am comforted that my heroes and heroines face these same questions. Early in 2018, my family visited the birthplace of Martin Luther King Jr. We explored his home where his dad fathered not only his biological family, but his human family. Here the community planned and prayed. Within these walls they advocated for equality and peace.

I was struck by the dining room table, the silverware that the King family used still in place. I imagined the prayers that echoed in that room, the conversations shared, and the encouragement given to one another.

As powerful as the King family home was, it was the Ebenezer Baptist Church that moved me spiritually. The ancient Irish Celts spoke of "thin space," where the veil between heaven and earth almost disappears—places like Lourdes or Mecca, where pilgrims gather to pray and to praise. To quote an Apache proverb, "Wisdom sits in [these] places."

As I entered the church where Martin Luther King Jr. worshiped, I felt as if going back in time. The old pews faced a simple podium, offset before a choir loft. Behind us a second level was filled with empty seats. Here King Jr. prayed and preached, and here his funeral was held.

Recorded gospel music echoed in this simple and beautiful space. I sat with my daughter and my wife. We didn't speak. We simply soaked in the Spirit. Then, to our surprise, a recording of one of King's sermons started to play, given at a rally in Memphis during a sanitation workers' strike. Near the end, King reminds the audience of the parable of The Good Samaritan.

Like the parable mentioned earlier, the message is to encounter the stranger. It isn't the religious leaders that stop, but the stranger of a different religion who helps the person in need. King, speaking to his own experience of encountering the stranger, and being the stranger, offered his own reality and humanity. He says this of the two who passed the man in need:

> But I'm going to tell you what my imagination tells me. It's possible that those men were afraid. You see, the Jericho Road is a dangerous road. I remember when Mrs. King and I were first in Jerusalem. We rented a car and drove from Jerusalem down to Jericho. And as soon as we got on that road I said to my wife, "I can see why Jesus used this as the setting for his parable." It's a winding, meandering road. It's really conducive for ambushing. You start out in Jerusalem, which is about twelve hundred . . . feet above sea level. And by the time you get down to Jericho fifteen or twenty minutes later, you're about twenty-two feet below sea level. That's a dangerous road. In the days of Jesus it came to be known as the "Bloody Pass." And you know, it's possible that the priest and the Levite looked over that man on the ground and wondered if the robbers were still around. Or it's possible that they felt that the man on the ground was merely faking, and he was acting like he had been robbed and hurt in order to seize them over there, lure them there for quick and easy seizure. And so the first question that the priest asked, the first question that the Levite asked was, "If I stop to help this man, what will happen to me?"
>
> But then the Good Samaritan came by, and he reversed the question: "If I do not stop to help this man, what will happen to him?" That's the question before you tonight. Not, "If I stop to help the sanitation work-

ers, what will happen to my job?" Not, "If
I stop to help the sanitation workers, what
will happen to all of the hours that I usually
spend in my office every day and every week
as a pastor?" The question is not, "If I stop
to help this man in need, what will happen
to me?" The question is, "If I do *not* stop to
help the sanitation workers, what will happen to them?" That's the question.[34]

This was King's last sermon. He was assassinated the
next day. Known as the "I've Been to the Mountaintop"
sermon, King. offers the human emotion of fear. But he
also offers the humanity, and the divinity, of love.

He concludes his talk in an eerie fashion as he shares
that if his life were to end, he was grateful. He was pro-
phetic. But he also shares a vision for peace and equality.
He shares a vision of love:

Well, I don't know what will happen now.
We've got some difficult days ahead. But it
really doesn't matter with me now, because
I've been to the mountaintop. And I don't
mind. Like anybody, I would like to live—a
long life; longevity has its place. But I'm not
concerned about that now. I just want to do
God's will. And He's allowed me to go up
to the mountain. And I've looked over. And
I've seen the Promised Land. I may not get
there with you. But I want you to know tonight, that we, as a people, will get to the
Promised Land. So, I'm happy, tonight. I'm
not worried about anything. I'm not fearing
any man. Mine eyes have seen the glory of
the coming of the Lord.[35]

On the night before he died, King shared about the
coming of the Lord, as Jesus proclaims in the passage from
Gospel of Mark at the beginning of this chapter. The Lord

has come, and the Lord, God, lives within you and within me. But, as this great preacher shared, we are not in the "Promised Land." This space is only possible when we can be people of love and peace. Where the color of our skin does not divide us, where our gender and sexual identity does not define us, and where our age, income, culture, or religion does not dictate our place in the world. This is God's dream for us all.

Closing Thoughts

This chapter invites you to see God's dream for creation. It isn't about fame or fortune. It is a dream of love that leads to peace: peace in our world, in our communities, and in our hearts.

The chapter began with the idea of kingdom and pointed out that God's kingdom is just. It is fair. It is love. You are called to live a life of love, caring for those who are hungry, thirsty, naked, sick, and imprisoned.

This chapter invites you to reflect on the lepers of your world. Who are they? How can you heal them and heal yourself?

This chapter also recognizes the burden of this lifestyle, especially as you emerge as a leader. You will be misunderstood. You will be criticized. You will be mocked.

Others will appreciate your dreams, and the courage you displayed in pursuing them. You will be valued, and you will inspire others to dream the same dream that runs through the veins of generations. Some will not understand, but for those that do, you can inspire as you have been inspired by the spiritual giants of human history.

As a society, both in the public square, in our religious traditions, and in our families, we hold up those individuals who lived a life of love. We recall anecdotes of them sharing their love, God's love, with us. This chapter explored some of those figures from the public and religious fronts, most especially Dr. Martin Luther King Jr. In a time of great unrest and injustice, King emerged with a message of justice, and a message of peace.

We too live in a time of unrest and injustice. You may not be called King, but you do have the King, your God, living within you. You can feel it with every heartbeat. With every breath. It is time for you to emerge from the shadows, and to be a voice in what surely can feel like wilderness.

The compass of your journey is pointing north. It is almost time to discover your unique gifts and talents, that will set you forth down a path of living your dreams, and to live a life of unconditional love.

PART II

DISCOVER

CHAPTER 4

JOY TO THE WORLD

In his poem "Final Curve" American poet Langston Hughes wrote:

When you turn the corner

And you run into yourself

Then you know that you have turned

All the corners that are left.[36]

That "running into yourself" takes time, and often the wrong turns become our greatest teacher. At eighty-seven, just before his death, Michelangelo is said to have uttered, "*Ancora imparo*" – "I am still learning."

This chapter invites you into a brief exploration on vocation. This will prepare you for future Appreciative Inquiry steps that will serve as a tool for your own self-reflection and action steps. Not only will you discover how God is inviting you to re-examine your life and your vocations, but you will also recognize how doing this can change the world.

Moving Toward Joy

Consider the idea of a spiritual ladder. The prophet Rumi saw life as a constant upward movement.[37] At the top is God, and your true self. As Rumi described it, "The ladder leads you to heaven."[38] We climb this ladder, gaining more and more insight into who we are. We come to appreciate our gifts and our talents. As we approach the top, we operate with heightened awareness. This is what Kohlberg described in his sixth and final stage of moral development, the person driven by universal ethical principles.[39] Kohlberg did not believe many people consistently operated on this level. The contemporary example of someone at this stage that my students always cite is St. Teresa of Calcutta. It seems almost unrealistic, but this stage is presented as a destination in every person's life journey.

At the top of the ladder that Rumi describes you receive an invitation to discover your true self. You must chip away at the social constructs and inner thoughts that keep you from fitting into society's boxes. You must imagine the world as it can be and pursue it as your imagination reveals the divine.

One of the best litmus tests for assessing your actions is joy. The familiar adage says, "when you love what you do, you never work a day in your life." The spirit of this notion speaks to living a life of joy. Consider what brings you joy, and you will gain insight into who you truly are, and how you should be spending your remaining days.

You may also consider where your daily life is lacking joy. This can provide lessons on what may need to change. I am often struck by the joylessness of the community where I live. Most mornings, I walk twenty minutes to work. In my busy Queens neighborhood, I see the mad rush to school and work. I see cars speeding, drivers yelling, people running. There is so much stress, anger, and frustration—and I must be careful not to fall into the same trap.

This early morning anxiety is partly due to people's lack of joy in life. There is a daily race to 5:00 pm, a weekly race to Friday, and a career race to retirement. We count down the hours and minutes, and we spend our life wishing it away. Imagine a day where the hours go too fast. This can occur only if you are doing what you love, in joy. You were never meant to speed to work, race against time, and see your life disappear. The younger generations seem to know how to slow down, how to be flexible, how to work together. The temptations of the world remain, but at least the young seem moved to examine work with creative, alternative solutions.

St. Teresa of Calcutta said, "Joy is prayer, joy is strength, joy is love, joy is a net of love by which you can catch souls."[40] This is what makes joy contagious—it captures the imagination of others. Take a moment to reflect on the joyful people in your life, past and present. Did they not exude love? St. Francis de Sales said, "Be who you are and be that well." Being who you are is to be joy. You are joy by doing what you love.

Are you doing what you love?

Joy as Vocation

My father is an electrician. He, I, and his family are beyond proud of the business he built and the people he helped along the way. Working for him when I was sixteen, during the summer between my first year and sophomore year in high school, I quickly learned two lessons. First: this task did not come easy for me, and it didn't intrigue me as it did my dad and my coworkers. I didn't mind the hard work (I didn't love it either), but making the lights go on was not my vocation. Second: my father worked even harder than I could imagine. I finally understood why he came home tired and often dirty. For that summer, I had to try walking in his boots. I didn't have to worry about meeting payroll, scheduling the employees, or daily responsibility. I did understand his work a little more, however, and that was a great gift. What I didn't understand then but came to understand and appreciate later in life was that he loved his work. He was good at it, worked hard, and learned constantly. It was his vocation, especially when he would get a call from a family in need.

In 2012, Hurricane Sandy destroyed significant parts of New York and New Jersey. My dad spent countless hours helping families who lost their electricity. He did the same in the heat of summer and the cold of winter when the extreme weather made his job even more difficult.

I am blessed to have a mother who also lived a vocation that brought her joy. She made sacrifices when she gave birth to twins, staying at home to raise us. As the father of a toddler, I do not understand how parents can raise multiple children. Talk about God's grace! I am flooded with memories of love that my mother shared as she still lives her vocation as a mother, and now grandmother. She held different professional positions, always staying true to her vocation in helping people in need. Most difficult and rewarding, however, was helping her children.

There isn't a Valentine's Day that I do not remember, but one from decades ago when my mom was very sick remains with me in a particular way. Usually she would buy me candy or tickets for upcoming New York Mets games. But when I was seven, it was a different kind of Valentine's Day. I recall hugging my frail mother before my father drove her to the hospital for surgery. I can still see the car leaving the driveway. She was sick for a few years, and it took some medical trial and error to determine that her spleen was not functioning properly and needed to be removed.

I cannot imagine how difficult it was for her. Sadly, many parents and grandparents who care for children face such difficulty. Many are and were much sicker than my mother was, and many did not have the same happy ending. Throughout my mother's illness, not once did I ever feel that she wasn't there to give love and to raise my sister and me. This can only be possible if it is a true vocation. It is only possible if there is joy.

We can have a deceptive impression of what joy really is. Joy isn't a fairy tale, or a happy-go-lucky state of mind. Joy may involve difficult days. It may not always be easy.

But for those who do what they love it is worthwhile. To quote Martin Luther King Jr. again:

> If a man is called to be a street sweeper, he should sweep streets even as a Michelangelo painted, or Beethoven composed music or Shakespeare wrote poetry. He should sweep streets so well that all the hosts of heaven and earth will pause to say, "Here lived a great street sweeper who did his job well." No work is insignificant. All labor that uplifts humanity has dignity and importance and should be undertaken with painstaking excellence.[41]

So, what is your vocation? In his book, *Let Your Life Speak*, author and teacher Parker Palmer writes, "Vocation does not mean a goal that I pursue. It means a calling that I hear. Before I can tell my life what I want to do with it, I must listen to my life telling me who I am."[42]

Listening to your life tell you who you are means to shift from listening to the voices of your past and present that tell you what to do and who to be. It can take a lifetime to clear out this noise, process the change, and make sense of your life. Be patient with yourself.

As you look back at your own journey, pay attention to what you recall. For example, one of my vocations is to write, and I can see how this was nourished, sharpened throughout my life. As I dig deeper into this reflection, I recall a memory from sophomore year in high school. My pastor, a great mentor, taught me the most important lesson of listening to the stories of others who may not have anyone else. Listening was the watchword for our parish youth ministry. I believe my writing is formed by this listening, strengthened by the movement of God in each of our lives.

Interesting enough, I also recall an anecdote from one of his homilies. I do not recall the scriptural passage upon which he was preaching, but I do recall him saying this to a friend who asked him to read a book that had written: "I am so sorry, I never realized you were in so much pain."

He shared that the author, who wrote a novel, not an autobiography, nevertheless revealed her own fears and insecurities. It was not her intention, but according to my pastor, it came through in her writing. I started to wonder, why does this stay with me all these years later?

As I grew as an author, I came to realize that I recalled an episode from decades ago so vividly because it touched upon my own insecurity. Insecurity was a chain that kept me from living my vocation fully. So, as I write and share my own vulnerabilities, I must also come to peace with the self-exposure that accompanies the writing. Through prayer, I learned that the healthy sharing of my vulnerabilities makes my writing more authentic, more relatable, and more important.

In my growing in my vocation, I continuously shed the old skin that without my realizing it keeps me from living the life God intends for me.

"Today I understand vocation quite differently—not as a goal to be achieved but as a gift to be received," said Palmer. "It comes from a voice 'in here' calling me to be the person I was born to be, to fulfill original selfhood given me at birth by God."[43]

Fulfilling your original selfhood will require you to slay monsters. You will deal with the voices of your past. Reflecting on the certain memories that "stick" is the first step in coming to peace. This is even more difficult when the voices are closest to us. I recommend that you seek spiritual direction or counseling so as to reflect with the support of a trusted, objective voice. Especially If you had an abusive parent or partner, you may need professional support to find peace. The damage caused by those closest to you can be crippling. However, it need not be permanent. But it may require more support and guidance than you may presently have. Many thoughtful and gifted people living their vocations as helpers are prepared to walk with you to a place of healing and peace.

As you claim your original selfhood, some may try to hold you back. While we pray that all in our inner circle would support and encourage your pursuit of your true self, some may struggle. Your transformation may require subtle changes such as reprioritizing the hours in your day. It may require greater changes such as leaving a job or moving to another location. You may need more training or formation in an area in which you are hoping to become an expert. You may need to make difficult decisions. If you are in a relationship, or an integral member of your family's system, this will require conversations, compromise, and support. It will not be easy, but it is worth it.

Remember, this is your birthright. This is your destiny. It is how God lives through you. It is God's dream for you. And it is God's dream for the community you live in. Living as your true self benefits not only you, it benefits others.

From 1971 to 1975 Dr. Wayne Dyer was an associate professor at St. John's University, the same institution where I was a student and where I currently teach and lead in ministry. His vocation called him to something larger than the campus he called home. The idea of tenure, a dream for many intelligent, caring people, was not his vocation. He felt called to something different, and for him, something more.

During my graduate studies, one of Dyer's students was my mentor. He recalled sitting in the cafeteria, listening to the professor share his early insights into the world and the human condition. Dyer was good at what he did, but his soul was taking him down a different journey. He took a chance, left the security of his position at St. John's, and in his station wagon with his family went on the road, selling his books from bookstore to bookstore. Through speaking engagements his audience grew, the right people came into his life, and his first book, *Your Erroneous Zones*, launched his career. An estimated thirty-five million people have read this book.

His vocation led him to a larger, global audience. Some professors find their vocation in reaching their students more intimately, in a classroom. One isn't better than the other. It is just a matter of what is one's calling, and in what brings people joy.

Dyer went on to publish more than forty books, twenty-one of them New York Times bestsellers. *This* was one of his vocations. He was also a father, a husband, a dear friend and guide to many. If you watch his online videos and read his books, you will feel the underlying sense of peace and joy that his work exudes. You are called to experience the same in your lives. And, like Dyer, you can help many others who will benefit from you sharing your gifts and talents.

Closing Thoughts

As this chapter concludes, we return to where it started. St. Francis de Sales said, "Be who you are, and be that well." Who are you? This chapter explored the ideas of joy, and vocation. It prepares you for the remainder of this book that will guide your own pursuit of your true self. The next two chapters explore the identification of your gifts and talents and invite you to discover what moves you. This process is intended to move you closer to discovering your true self, and to live a life of joy rooted in God's unconditional love.

CHAPTER 5

YOUR GIFTS AND TALENTS

Humanity is like a large puzzle; each of us is a piece. Each of us has our own curves and edges—our unique gifts and talents. When those gifts and talents are assembled, together they create something beautiful.

Often, it is tragedy that brings the puzzle pieces together. In the days following September 11, 2001, humanity showed its best, acknowledging our connection in the face of extreme horror and death. Barriers crumbled and distractions became meaningless.

The same can be said for the many other natural disasters, terrorist attacks, acts of violence, and fatal accidents. Communities unite, raising their voices in prayer and sharing love.

Sadly, these initial moments of healing can be brief. Distractions return, priorities shift, and life moves back to its accustomed normal. Love of brother and sister is no longer the priority. To-do lists, bank accounts, and self-gain again come to the fore.

Imagine if life was different. Imagine if we reflected upon the world around us and attended to God's movement in our lives. Imagine if we responded to the violence and pain throughout the world, not just in our own town. Imagine if we kept our priorities straight.

God gives you the tools to respond. You can change the world. You possess gifts and talents that you do not fully recognize nor appreciate. This chapter invites you to discover those gifts and talents. By answering five questions, you will gain insight into how you tick, and how you are meant to live your one precious life.

You may be inspired by one of my heroes, St. Vincent de Paul. I first encountered his story in grade school when I read about his love for the poor. This was reinforced whenever I passed a donation box in our church for the St. Vincent de Paul Society, which used the collections to feed the poor of the community.

When I came to St. John's University as a student, I learned more about Vincent. He continues to teach me how to live, how to use my gifts and talents. Many books, reflections, and videos capture his spirit. Our short reflection will demonstrate how by being attentive and by having the courage to respond, you can change the world.

A Soul named Vincent

Vincent did not seek Catholic priesthood to become a saint. Sure, he had intentions to help people, and he felt a strong relationship with God, but his main motivation was security. It was not purely self-centered. During the tumultuous seventeenth-century France, if you were a priest, you were granted stability, and so were your parents.

Throughout his life Vincent had a series of conversion moments, but only when he began to reflect on his past did he come to understand how God's hand was moving through him and through others. Later he could see how, beginning with an encounter with Jesus in the poor, he set forth on an extraordinary journey, a life that history would recall as holy and as a revelation of God's love.

In 1617 Vincent had two specific conversion moments that continue to impact millions of lives. The first was hearing a dying servant's confession. The man was asking for God's forgiveness, searching for peace. Vincent was moved by this experience, so much so that, reflecting on this encounter, he realized that he had truly encountered Jesus in that man. He saw the divinity that lived within him, and within all of us.

Vincent was also moved that those who worked the land lacked a real relationship with God. Moved by the dying man, Vincent dedicated his life to serving the poor by being the face of God for them. And he was good at it. He was also troubled by it, and one conversation with Madame de Gondi, a friend, played a critical role in transforming his life. His concern for the poor overwhelmed him, and after he expressed to de Gondi how his heart was moved, she asked him, "What must be done?"

This transformative question launched Vincent's vocation. He soon discovered his gift for oratory. When he spoke, people listened. Eight months after his experience with the dying man, Vincent had a second conversion experience.

One Sunday before Mass, he learned of a family that needed food and medicine. He told the congregation of this need and later that day it became clear that people had listened. The same people who earlier had filled the pews were lining up down the block, giving what little that they had to help the needy family.

This generosity presented a new problem. So many items were donated that perishable goods started to go bad. There was a need for organization, and here Vincent discovered another gift—he could bring people together in an organized fashion.

Three days after Vincent had asked help for this family, he formed what would be called the Confraternity of Charity. Mostly women, these people came to help the poor. Vincent soon had other individuals enter his life, like St. Louise de Marillac, who shared his vision and ministry to serve the poor.

Vincent used his gifts to change the face of the poor in France. He could spend one day with the royalty and leadership of France, and the next with those who called the streets home. Interestingly, Vincent wore the same clothes for both encounters, reminding the rich of the needs of the poor.

That question that de Gondi proposed to Vincent, "What must be done," became known as *the Vincentian question*. The communities Vincent founded and that still serve the poor today answer the same question. Inspired by a man who used his gifts to help those most in need, major institutions of higher education, religious communities, and non-profit organizations now serve in innovative and substantial ways, allowing others to use their gifts and talents to respond to the cries of the poor.

Vincent believed in collaboration—its Latin roots mean "to labor together." While he gets much of the credit, he did nothing alone. He built communities that allowed for shared leadership.

Vincent labored together with those who helped him serve and with those whom he served. Those he served taught him how he and his collaborators could best serve them—a key aspect of the Vincentian charism. Together, they labored in the difficult and sacrificial work of serving one another with unconditional love. This work continues to this day.

This example is one of many. So much good comes about in our world because of individuals like Vincent. Their names may be unknown, their stories not told, but their love echoes through eternity.

Your Gifts and Talents

This next part of this chapter poses a question, the fundamental question. *What are your gifts and talents?*

You see, your gifts and talents include two features:

1. You possess them while others may not, and
2. Your gifts are meant for you to share.

One of the most powerful passages in Christian scripture is in St. Paul's first letter to the Corinthians:

> Now there are varieties of gifts, but the same Spirit; and there are varieties of services, but the same Lord; and there are varieties of activities, but it is the same God who activates all of them in everyone. To each is given the manifestation of the Spirit for the common good. To one is given through the Spirit the utterance of wisdom, and to another the utterance of knowledge according to the same Spirit, to another faith by the same Spirit, to another gifts of healing by the one Spirit, to another the working of miracles, to another prophecy, to another the discernment of spirits, to another various kinds of tongues, to another the interpretation of tongues. All these are activated by one and the same Spirit, who allots to each one individually just as the Spirit chooses. (1Cor 12:4-12)

This text, thousands of years old, describes the different gifts one can possess. Inspired by my mentor and colleague, Bro. Mike Sheerin, F.M.S., I wonder what an updated version could look like. I imagine it could read something like this:

> To one there is given through the Spirit the gifts of listening, to another gifts of laughter, to another gifts of writing, to another gifts of parenthood, to another gifts of teaching, to another gifts of research, to another gifts of making electricity, to another gifts of healing wounds, to another the gifts of listening and encountering, to another gifts of protecting society, to another gifts of advocating for justice and equality, to another gifts of organizing, to another gifts of

motivating, to another gifts of comforting the mourning, to another gifts of cleaning, cooking, and maintaining, to another gifts of bringing peace into hostile lands.

This litany can go on and on, reflecting the different vocations we as a society possess. Your gifts are not arbitrarily assigned. Your gifts and talents are for you, and for you to use them appropriately for others' benefit. Many in our society misuse their gifts. Some political leaders use their gift of rhetoric and power to line their pockets and serve the wealthy, instead of those on the margins. Some religious leaders take advantage of the vulnerable. Some appear as leaders, only to serve themselves, not others, and some ask for our trust, only to break it. Throughout human history, generations have suffered when talents and gifts are misused.

It is disappointing when gifts and talents are misused; it is also disappointing when talents go to waste. Imagine Michelangelo choosing not to create because of society's pressure or narrative. Imagine Francis of Assisi listening to his father and spending his life selling fabrics. Imagine Rumi never writing, or Gandhi never speaking. Imagine Dorothy Day never opening her home and her heart to the poor. Imagine Martin Luther King Jr. not giving his sermons or not sharing his dreams for racial equality. Imagine your heroes never giving you the time of day, words of encouragement, life lessons, or love.

You possess unique gifts and talents. Like these great leaders, you can live an extraordinary life. Just remember why you were made.

Closing Thoughts

The lessons about past and present leaders using their gifts and talents are inspiring. You are not called to do it *their* way. You are called to do it *your* way—responding to the needs of the world in the way only *you* can.

The next chapter will invite you into a deeper reflection, to discover perhaps hidden aspects of who you are, including your deepest joys and hopes for yourself and for the world. You will tap into your unique gifts and talents, and you will better recognize how God made you to change the world.

CHAPTER 6

FIVE QUESTIONS

So, what are your gifts and talents?

Surely you have many, but it may be difficult at first to recognize and to appreciate them truly. Throughout this chapter, we will reflect on the following five questions:

1. What is your earliest memory of being happy?

2. What is your earliest memory of doing something you love?

3. If you could do one thing every day, what would it be?

4. What have other people praised you for, in your past and in your present?

5. If you could change the world, how would you do it?

You may try to answer these questions quickly, but I advise you to give this time.

First, find a quiet space that avoids interruptions. Second, do not rush through the memories. Take a pen and paper and reflect on each question. Third, be free in how you reflect. You may wish to journal your memory, describing it in detail. You may decide to draw the memory. For example, as I reflected on a childhood holiday, I drew the dining room and kitchen where we celebrated Christmas Eve. I made note of where family members—some living, others deceased—once sat. I recalled where the tree stood, and where we set up the food. I left this activity comforted by my past blessings. I also recognized why as a father I continue to put such value on this holiday. I want my daughter to feel the same joy and comfort that I experienced, as I too want to recapture some of that memory.

This invitation to reflect is an intimate process. It may bring up mixed emotions, so be patient and work through them well. Share your emotions with trusted mentors and spiritual directors. This does not have to be a journey you take alone.

If you get stuck or feel difficult emotions, ask yourself: "Why am I feeling this way?" Both positive and negative emotions and memories can, if processed, generate gratitude and healing.

This chapter explores these five questions in greater detail and focus. They are characteristic of the Discover step of Appreciative Inquiry. Allow them to prepare you for the next steps, in which you will be invited to dream and to bring those dreams to life.

Following each question, I will share my own reflections as a way of modeling the process, while also revealing a bit more of myself as a fellow pilgrim on this journey. I am excited for you as you enter this process of reflection. I pray you gain greater insight into how you are wonderfully made, while recognizing your best response to the needs of this world.

What is your earliest memory of being happy?

Reflecting on these questions will give you greater insight into your past, present, and future. The first question invites you to recall a time you felt happy. Try to dig deep into your earliest of memories.

Guiding Questions:

- What was the scene?
- Who was there?
- What do your senses remember—what did you smell and how did it feel?
- Were you eating? If so, what does it taste like?
- If you were touching someone or something, what does it feel like?
- Who made you happy? How does it feel?
- What do you see? Describe the details?
- What did this happiness feel like? What does it feel like now?
- Why did this memory come back into your consciousness?

Insights:

Reflecting on my earliest memory of being happy, I recall one Saturday night waiting to watch my favorite television show, "ALF," a sitcom about an alien that came to live with a welcoming family after his spaceship crashed. I remember holding my ALF doll as I watched in the living room. I even remember having Chinese food delivered earlier that night, and my parents sitting in the kitchen drinking coffee while my sister and I watched the show.

I felt safe. I was happy as my favorite show was on and my family was home.

Upon reflection, I believe this memory came into my consciousness because it was something I simply enjoyed. It was a show that made me laugh. In my life, I remain a fan of silly and unrealistic comedy and television series (like this one about an alien). In many ways, television, like sports, is a healthy escape that allows me to rest. In this memory, I learn a little more about myself, and the way I function. Even to this day, getting lost in a baseball game or in a television series keeps me smiling and present when I am with others. It helps me recognize my introvert needs and how I must find time each day to rest so I can be my best self.

Your reflection on this first question can give you greater insight into yourself. Once you have this insight, watch how you start to recognize new patterns and behaviors. You will appreciate aspects of yourself. For example, after reflecting on this question and recalling the above memory, I had an experience one night after returning home from work late, around 9:30. After catching up with my wife, I stared at the blank television. I couldn't recall a night when I didn't watch television before going to sleep, other than when we were out on a date or for some special occasion.

There is no good or bad judgement that accompanies these memories; rather, it reveals a daily behavior I use to relax and unwind. I did not recognize this as clearly as I did before this reflection, and I am thankful for it. I am also challenged whether this is the best way to reflect at the end of the day. Could some of this time, or all of it, be used to pray, reflect, and write? I am in no rush to change the behavior, just to be more aware about myself.

I also recognize the safety that I felt in this memory. My parents were in the kitchen, my sister was on the couch. I believe my grandmother and uncle were present too. I do not take for granted the roof over my head, the full belly, and the presence of loved ones that made an innocent child free to lose himself in a silly sitcom.

What is your earliest memory of doing something you love?

I love this question, and I equally love posing it to participants in Appreciative Inquiry workshops that I facilitate.

I enjoy watching their faces as they share their memories with the larger group after they take the time to go down memory lane. It is as if a dimmed spark is now shining brighter.

In responding to this question, once again dig deep into your memory. Like before, focus on these guiding questions:

- What was the scene?
- Who was there?
- What senses do you remember—what did you smell and how did it feel?
- What were you doing?
- What did this happiness feel like? What does it feel like now?
- When was the last time you did this activity?

Insights:

As I answer this question for myself, I remember when I was around seven or eight years old. I was in my bedroom. I loved to draw Warner Brothers and Disney cartoon characters directly on the wall, as if it was my own personal blank canvas. One day I started to draw on the walls, and in no time, I had a mural full of recognizable characters like Bugs Bunny, the Tasmanian Devil, and Goofy. Amazingly, my parents allowed me the space to express my creativity.

I can recall their friends who challenged their parenting practices. I also remember when my father painted over the wall. After I had grown older my then-teenaged self no longer appreciated a wall of cartoons. I also remember how difficult it was for my dad as the cartoons kept seeping through the layers of new paint. He did this with love, as it was worth it for his son to be happy.

I now watch my daughter, Shea. She loves books. She would pick a book instead of any toy. Even when she was only a year old, she would sit by herself, turn the pages, and be amused by the drawings. My wife and I wonder what this will mean for her as she gets older. She also loves to draw and to express herself creatively. She colors with a deep intensity and laser focus. Who is this little child of God? In time, we will find out.

This question intends to help you remember what you loved doing a long time ago. Perhaps this was the start to a vocation that you pushed to the side. Or, maybe this is an insight that can become a new joy, either as a full-time job or as an on-going project. Perhaps you are still doing what you loved when you were a child. If so, how special it is that you remain committed to this calling and expression of your spirit.

These earliest memories reveal what is unique to our true self. Once again, one memory may open a floodgate of memories. Think of this as your soul trying to shine a light into your world.

Society forms a shell over us that keeps us from seeing our true self. These memories can crack that shell, revealing our true self to us on a very intimate level.

Isn't it fascinating that your future may be revealed by looking into your past? How ironic that we spend our early years trying to grow up, but if we are wise, we spend our adult years trying to reconnect with our younger, innocent, and true self.

Children remind us of how to be our true self. I love watching my daughter around other children. She is fascinated by them, as most toddlers are when encountering someone else like them. They see something bright in the other person.

At the conclusion of yoga sessions, participants will often recite, "The light in me sees the light in you. Namaste." Children model this witness to the light in their interactions.

During our daughter's first two years, my wife would take her to the public library for a music and movements class. The children play with instruments, scarves, and shapes, all directed by a patient teacher who uses music in the background.

I recall one morning watching this controlled chaos. My daughter joined the other children in sharing instruments. She watched an older kid as he used an instrument in a way she never imagined. Another child used the shape that my daughter recently discarded. A room of thirty-plus kids moved from object to object, quietly observing one another. As the comfort built, some held hands, while others kept an eye on their parent. They co-exist, they learn, they grow.

What most fascinates me is that they do not share the same concerns that adults do when entering a new community. Toddlers do not worry about what they wear, what they say, or how they should act. They just are themselves. And they are encouraged by the light within others: some guide, some teach, and some inspire in their reciprocal relationship. Another lesson for us, who in growing up have left the child in us behind.

If you could do one thing every day, what would it be?

This question speaks to your vocation, your calling. It invites you to explore who you are, and what you were meant to do in your short time on earth.

Guiding Questions:

- What would this look like for you?
- How would you feel?

- Does your life currently include any aspect of this action?
- How could you begin to include this in your life?

Insights:

In eighth grade, we were asked to describe for the yearbook what we wanted to do when we were older. My response was to be a cartoonist. That same desire from my thirteen-year-old self remains—not in the form of doodles, but in simply creating. This takes different forms. When I paint or draw, I remain open to the movement of the Spirit. When I write, I invoke the Spirit and allow inspiration to guide my thoughts and sentences. When I speak publicly, I invoke the Spirit in choosing my thoughts and words. When I work on projects to guide students in their faith journey, I invoke the Spirit to move my thoughts, words, and actions. I am creating as an instrument of God.

Chiara Lubich, founder of the Focolare Movement, a lay organization dedicated to peace, spiritual renewal, and ecumenical dialogue. She describes being God's instrument in this way:

> A pen never knows what it will write, a brush never knows what it will paint and a chisel never knows what it will sculpt. When God takes someone into his hands in order to accomplish a new work in his Church, the person doesn't know what she will do. I think this might be my case: I'm only the tool.[44]

Lubich considered herself to be only an instrument of unity. As a Catholic lay leader, she trained as a teacher, but was called by God to a deeper spiritual life. During World War II, she and others gathered in air-raid shelters to read scripture. In war-stricken Europe she worked to care for the poor and so built up unity. Her response to the needs

of the world and to the urging of God generated a movement now active in over 182 countries with millions of followers. Her vocation was to be an instrument of God like
the Blessed Mary who, in her yes, brought Christ into the
world.

As I explore my own vocation as God's instrument, I am
reminded that on those days when I do not create, I feel as
if I am losing and wasting time. I feel tired and defeated.
My soul in a way is crushed. That is not the way we are
meant to live.

I felt most fulfilled when, at the end of the day, I rest
my head on my pillow and feel most alive because I had
been in service to others. It is the secret of our holy moth-
ers and fathers who truly lived by dedicating their lives to
service. Some surrender their lives to service completely,
responding to the needs of others rather than their own.
Lesser-known angels in disguise find ways to make a positive impact on others. Some do this by treating those they
supervise with compassion; others give of their free time to
mentor and coach young people. Some volunteer at nurs-
ing homes and hospitals; others spend their time, day in
and day out, preparing healthy meals for their loved ones.
This question of vocation may require simple changes, or
changes in perspective. But it may require a radical change
in your life.

A final thought that relates to your perspective on life.
As you focus on what you do, do not forget that you are,
as Henri Nouwen reminds us, "God's beloved." How you
spend your days is an opportunity to glorify God by your
actions, your prayer, and your relationships. What you do
and how you do it are secondary to knowing that you truly
belong to God.

Nouwen writes: "We are not what we do, we are not
what we have, we are not what others think of us. Coming
home is claiming the truth. I am the beloved child of a loving creator."[45]

The question of how to spend your day in an ideal world invites you to return home to God, to see yourself first as God's beloved. Then, and only then, can you look at your days through these holy eyes and to allow your actions to flow from this reality.

As Lubich modeled, once your perspective changes, you allow the Spirit to move you into a ministry of love that can fill all your days and the days of others.

What have other people praised you for, in your past and in your present?

Earlier we explored the "I Am" narrative, and how we often speak negatively of ourselves. We say, "I am not good at this"; "I am not as qualified or good looking as another"; or "I am not good enough."

God reveals his name to Moses as "I Am." Since you are made in God's image, if "I Am" is followed by something negative, it cannot be true. As an attentive spiritual seeker, you will find your spiritual growth in discovering and understanding your uniqueness, your exceptional gifts and talents.

Although we may be hardest on ourselves, God's angels are often at work for us in the form of others. There are people who have complimented you in the past and in the present. Sometimes you do not hear it, or you dismiss it. Even if you have processed it, you may focus on the negativity spoken to you in the past. The challenge is to hold on to compliments as small gifts from God. They reveal something true about you.

Take time to reflect on what others have praised you for, in your past and in your recent days.

Guiding Questions:

- What compliments did you receive as a child?
- As a teenager?
- As an adult?
- How did you feel?
- Do you believe it?

Insights:

All my life, people have complimented me for my writing. It started in grammar school with a teacher's praise for my essays. In high school, I received awards and words of encouragement for my work with the school paper. In college, when I initially majored in journalism, I could see how my talents made the subject easy for me. In math class, I needed extra help. In writing courses, I finished earlier than everyone else. I seemed to have a natural gift that had been cultivated throughout my teenage years by writing for many publications, even a local newspaper.

As I moved away from writing, I would still experiment with websites and other creative expressions. I often received compliments, but I did not always listen. Only recently could I accept the fact that I needed to write this book and to dedicate time every day to my website so as to shine a bit of God's love into world growing ever more divided.

As I committed time to write more deeply and more often, the words continued to flow. I marvel at this process as it is now a daily spiritual experience.

And as I reflect on my life, I remember those mentors, family, and friends who all along were telling me that I am a writer. While I did not always listen, at every turn those voices were pointing me to write and to use this gift to glorify God and to change our world. At a time when many loud voices distract and divide us, I feel called to unite by the power of the pen, inspired by listening to the God that lives within and the God that lives within others—especially those suffering and on the margins.

I followed the journalism track to St. John's University, but in time changed my major to psychology as I felt called to help others using other gifts, those of listening and asking reflective questions. This led me into a deeper spirituality, a path of helping, and in time, spiritual writing.

Whatever road we may be traveling, God meets us there, inviting us to know God and to use our gifts and talents. Allow me to provide one additional personal anecdote. After high school I had moved away from art to pursue journalism and then psychology. Nevertheless, during the summer between my sophomore and junior year I was invited to use my painting skills in an unexpected and life-changing way.

After volunteering the previous year at a children's hospital, over the summer I was hired to work with resident patients, primarily in the recreation room. My main responsibility was to entertain the children healthy enough to leave their rooms. I would make sure all the toys were cleaned and put away after use. Somewhere along the way, I painted a Spiderman mural for some of the children. The Spiderman movie was extremely popular at the time, and the kids were excited to see my depiction. This painting then led to a difficult and meaningful request.

A few doors from the recreation room a teenager, Leah, was approaching the end of her life. Her family and her doctors decided to remove her breathing tubes and Leah was not expected to live beyond three days. The staff asked me to paint an image on her wall.

For the next three days, across from Leah's bed, I painted a large, colorful tree. Sometimes her mom would be present, as would nurses and other colleagues. I struggled with the decision that the parents and the hospital had made, not fully understanding why they wanted me to do this. The staff was offered counseling to help us process the experience together.

So I painted as a way of doing something for Leah. Most of the time, only she and I were in the room. With each brushstroke I would describe what I was painting. At other times, I would be silent as meditative music filled the room. She would stare in my direction and I would respond with a smile. As each branch took shape, I felt closer to her. At first I was a stranger, but over those few days I felt a connection to this person, only a few years younger than I was, but who had suffered enough for a lifetime.

I invited my colleagues to join me in the painting. I asked them to draw leaves on the branches. In short time, a variety of styles and colors filled the tree. The wall reflected the love of this community. I had not chosen to use my artistic talent as a profession, but looking back I find great peace that I could be God's instrument to make a dark situation a little brighter. I also pray that my artistic expression helped Leah as she transitioned home to her loving God.

As you reflect on your life, consider what was celebrated, what came easier, what brought you joy. These memories are spiritual breadcrumbs for your own discovery of your true self.

One of my favorite stories about St. Francis is that before he dedicated his life to serving the poor he enjoyed throwing parties and hanging out with others. His singing late at night with his friends would wake up the neighbors. I can picture this young man and his peers walking through their medieval town after a night of friendship and maybe even some wine. People would yell from the window for Francis to be quiet, but he took no heed, because he felt happy.

Later in life, he would still be singing, still with friends but not while returning from a party. Instead, he and his peers (some from that original group he hung out with before his conversion) were returning from a day dedicated to

serving the poor. This time his song was different. He sang
to praise God, like he did in his *Canticle of the Sun*, or while
he and his companions were knocking on doors asking for
food to feed the hungry. The song had changed, but Francis still was singing.

Consider these words from the Rig Veda, the oldest of
the Hindu sacred scriptures:

> *Sing the song of celestial love, O singer!*
>
> *May the divine fountain of eternal grace and joy*
> *enter your soul.*
>
> *May Brahma, (the Divine One),*
>
> *Pluck the strings of your inner soul*
>
> *With His celestial fingers,*
>
> *And feel His own presence within.*
>
> *Bless us with a divine voice*
>
> *That we may tune the harp-strings of our life*
>
> *To sing songs of Love to you.*[46]

What song are you singing?

What brought you joy in younger years, and now, years
later, how does that still reveal itself?

So much can be revealed from our past to inform our
present and our future. What did others see in you that was
bright? How can you light that candle again, or as Rig Veda
states, how can you sing songs of love to God?

If you could change the world, how would you do it?

I am fascinated by politics. I am also constantly disappointed. Leaders who campaigned on promises to make con-
crete changes in law and society often fail to do so out of
their own self-interest, especially when they are seeking to
be re-elected and to maintain power.

We live in a political era where the search for truth is not clear. Every commentator and network has its spin, and although much is unknown, it is known that the rich get richer and the poor get poorer. The one clear thing is that many charged with changing the world only make changes that benefit themselves.

It is easy to feel frustrated. Despite the world's corruption and selfishness, God still invites us to seek change. We should recall our own power, and the opportunity to change the world that lives within our own hearts, homes, and communities. This question invites you into a deeper exploration and reminder of the power within you.

If you could change the world, how will you do it?

Guiding Questions:

- What are societal injustices that hurt your heart?
- What are situations in your personal and professional life that upset and bother you?
- What can you change?
  - In these situations?
  - In your thoughts and actions?
  - In your perspective?

Insights:

Earlier, I described my experience at the childhood home of Dr. Martin Luther King Jr., especially the table where the King family gathered for meals. I was equally struck by the parlor where King's father facilitated community. While those in the state capitol and White House did what politicians often do, the community was moving together to advocate for their own rights and their neighbors'. I can imagine King Jr. watching his dad and those who sat in his home strategizing a peaceful demonstration for equal rights. An upstairs room was dedicated to the community, specifically women giving birth.

His home took in not only the King family, but the entire human family. Outside his front windows, King Jr. would have seen the homeless and hungry in the small field across the street. While he went to bed with a full stomach, just feet away others did not. This formed him and led him toward working to change the world.

I am a big fan of country music, and of all the musical acts my favorite is the duo Sugarland. One of their hits, *Happy Ending*, refers to Dr. King and Astronaut Neil Armstrong, and our own desire that our lives have a happy ending. Consider these lyrics:

> *And for all the dreams who have come and gone*
>
> *Who have reached for the stars, who have overcome?*
>
> *You're the hope, you're the wish, you're the truth.*
>
> *Baby, here's the proof*
>
> *Baby's born in the ghetto*
>
> *Baby's born with a silver spoon*
>
> *One tells his mama, "I'll have a dream."*
>
> *One tells his mama, "I'll walk the moon."*[47]

I appreciate how this song, released almost forty years after King's life was sacrificed in his dream for equality, continues to echo through time. While some consider King's dream for racial equality to be dead, there are armies of people who have the gifts and the courage to bring his dream to fruition—despite the great challenges and at times, darkness of our fellow humanity.

We often reference King, Mother Teresa, Dorothy Day, Buddha, Francis of Assisi, Gandhi, Chiara Lubich, Mohammed, Moses, and other spiritual leaders, not only because they lived life well, but because they were faithful to their true self. It encourages us as it re-ignites the flame of heroism within us.

We may never give speeches at the National Mall or be profiled on national news. We may never receive a national honor, or even be cited in a book or an article. This does not matter. What does matter is a life well-lived, a life for us and for others.

To change the world, to have real purpose, you must begin with what Henri Nouwen called his "growing conviction:"

Nouwen writes, "My life belongs to others just as much as I belong to myself, and that what is experienced as most unique often proves to be most solidly embedded in the common condition of being human.[48]"

We all share the same purpose—to leave the world a little better because we lived.

We do this by the gifts and talents that God gives us, and while we are unique, every other person also has unique gifts and talents. For every King Jr., there are the thousands who marched with him. For every Francis of Assisi, there are his companions, named and unnamed. For every Mother Teresa of Calcutta, there are those who served with her every day, those who were served and who loved, and those who have served and continue to serve the poorest of the poor. For every Buddha, there are those disciples that seek the same enlightenment and impact. For every Lubich there are millions who share her desire for unity and peace. Some are called to be the face of a movement, but most of us are called to be faithful and compassionate.

These are the teachers who mentor, the coaches who lead, the public servants who protect all, and the parents and grandparents, uncles and aunts, who comprise the village that is raising the next generation. These are the spiritual leaders, the friendly smiles, the first responders. These are the financially secure who give back, and the financially limited who give the little that they have. These are the members of the human family to which we belong.

We strive to mend what is broken and to celebrate and continue the best of our society. We find our purpose not in the brand of our shirt or car, or the size of our house or bank account, but in the joy of serving others and the joy of being true to our equally unique and common human spirit.

Closing Thoughts

This chapter invited you to explore five Discovery questions, leading you into a greater appreciation of who you truly are and to recognize the needs of the world. The next part focuses on identifying and embracing God's dream for you.

PART III

DREAM

CHAPTER 7

UNDERSTANDING GOD'S DREAMS

You have dreams. In fact, you have many dreams. They are the hopes and desires living in the depth of your soul. It is God speaking to you at your core, guiding you only if you will listen.

This part will guide you into the next process of Appreciative Inquiry, known as the Dream step. This step invites you to recognize your dreams, understand them, and then prepare yourself to implement aspects of these desires.

We begin with a deeper reflection on dreams in general.

Dreams are common in scripture and spirituality. They serve as a gateway of communication between God and creation. Joseph (with his amazing technicolor dream coat) dreamed of his future leadership in Egypt (Gen 37:5). The angel Gabriel appeared in a dream to Joseph, to whom Mary was betrothed, revealing the truth of her conception (Mt 1:18-25). Dreams urge you to a deeper relationship with God and with others.

We also have dreams for our lives. We hope and imagine a better, just world, not only for ourselves, but for our world.

At a key point every fall during my first-year seminar I ask the students to look out the window.

"Look outside and what do you see," I ask.

"Planes," "cars," "New York City skyline," "cement," lacrosse field," "houses," are just a few of the common responses.

"All that you see was once a person's dream," I respond.

Leonardo DaVinci dreamed of a flying machine. In 1903, 420-plus years after DaVinci put pen to paper, the Wright brothers shared the same dream, and their "Flyer" lifted from level ground in North Carolina.

Every car, building, structure, and home was once a dream. Leaders made them reality. Dreams are built on the shoulders of dreamers who came before, and future dreamers will stand on your shoulders.

Like my students, most of us take what we see for granted. We see a plane and cannot imagine a vessel that weights tens of thousands of pounds flying above the birds and clouds. As there was a need for a better and quicker mode of transportation, a dream was born.

There are countless needs in our world, just waiting for a dream to become a solution.

Can we walk down a city street and imagine a world where fellow humans no longer call a cardboard box their home?

Can we find solutions to social issues of injustice, be they local, national, or global?

Can we be instruments of peace in a divided, hostile world?

It begins with a dream. The dream you experience in your sleep and the dreams you experience in your hearts inspire this next part that allows God to speak to you and through you

Dreams, conscious and unconscious, provide an important step in the Appreciative Inquiry process. As discussed earlier, Appreciative Inquiry looks at the best of an institution, group, or person, but dreaming allows for creativity and introspection. First comes discovery (the questions explored in the last chapter are rooted in this model), then the dream step offers opportunities for continued self-discovery, while also leading you into action.

This dream step can be difficult because as individuals and as a group, we find ourselves "boxed in," limited by constraints.

Consider what Thomas Merton says about placing limits on our spirit:

> Why do we spend our lives striving to be something that we would never want to be, if only we knew what we wanted? Why do we waste our time doing things which, if we only stopped to think about them, are just the opposite of what we were made for?[49]

The past chapter explored the critical questions that reveal what you are made for in this life. The remainder of this book leads you to make changes that will transform not only you but the world.

Will it matter when you die?

One word of caution: pay attention to the inner voice of defeat that says, "You can't do this." This negative voice moves freely, and you must make the intentional, sometimes exhausting, effort to dismiss that narrative.

Making that effort is what I believe Jesus meant when he said, "Away with you, Satan!" (Mt 4:8). I struggle with the notion of evil and the devil. As I have grown deeper spiritually, I have come to understand this differently. I see evil, or sin, as something that keeps us from God. When we treat others, and ourselves, with anything less than respect, dignity, and love, we are keeping ourselves away from God. This is sin.

In the same spirit, when we do not commit our life to what we are made for, is this not also sinful? This does feel dramatic, and somewhat uncomfortable to write, but there is an urgent seriousness to our life and how we live it. Not only because of its impact in our own life, but in others' lives, too.

Imagine how many are waiting for you to live the life you were meant to live.

This Dream step contains an important distinction.

Dreams worth pursuing cannot be superficial or external. The pot of gold at the end of the rainbow is not of this world. Money offers a false promise, as do those things that boost your ego and false self.

God's dream for you is internal. It must transform you, and then, in return, transform others. Yes, money used well can do good in this world. But dreaming of riches, or of having the biggest house or the fastest car, is not God's dream for you. As you dream, ask yourself this question: *Will it matter when I die?*

The answer will help you distinguish what is of this world, and what is of God. Temptations for power, fame, and fortune are not of this world. You can't take any of those with you.

Avoiding Temptations

Let's turn our attention to a more familiar episode from the Gospels, the story of Jesus in the desert. After being baptized by his cousin, John, Jesus prepared for his active ministry by going to the desert for forty days to fast and pray. Experts believe Jesus died at the age of thirty-three, and he started his ministry at the age of thirty. The good that he did (that we are aware of) came about only in a three-year span, and his ministry began with his temptation in the desert.

Jesus taking thirty years to prepare for his active ministry is an important reminder to all of us. Dreams take time to reveal themselves, and you may need to prepare yourself by facing challenges and experiencing different turns on the road of life.

Apart from a few stories from his childhood, we do not know what this time of preparation was like for Jesus. But we do is that Jesus, as he started his ministry, faced great temptations.

Here you are, ready to dream, and perhaps, ready to breathe new life into the world. You, like Jesus, must be prepared for the temptations.

Are your dreams of God?

The external rewards with which Jesus is tempted three times are like the worldly distractions that may influence your decisions and focus.

Do you respond to your God, who wants you to be at peace and to bring love to all, or do you respond to your ego, which is looking to feed itself upon what society says is important? Jesus confronts this same reality—temptations to satisfy hunger, to exercise power, and to accumulate wealth. Let's explore these temptations and reflect on how they can indicate whether the dreams we pursue are of and for God.

Temptation #1: Hunger

Jesus' first temptation is to turn stone into bread.

Jesus replies, "It is written: 'One does not live by bread alone but by every word that comes from the mouth of God'" (Mt 4:4). Immediate satisfaction would not be worth the larger consequences.

Imagine how hungry you would be after forty days. When I fast for religious observances, I can feel the hunger by noon. Just imagine Jesus' hunger when he faced this temptation. At times, in searching for your dreams, you will be hungry—not just for food, but also for desires. There are no shortcuts. Facing such hungers will take time and patience. If it is of God, your time in the desert will be worthwhile.

Temptation #2: Identity

The second temptation brings Jesus to the pinnacle of the temple. The devil challenges him to cast himself down, trusting that the angels will save him. Jesus is tempted to show his power and his greatness. If he would take such a public risk and be saved, surely people would know how special he is. Of course, if Jesus were to do this, he would be responding to the devil's will, not God's. God never asked Jesus to make a spectacle. In fact, throughout scripture, Jesus often tells those he heals to not say who is responsible. The devil begins this temptation saying, "If you are the Son of God, throw yourself down" (Mt 4:6), but Jesus does not reveal his identity. He responds, "Do not put the Lord your God to the test" (Mt 4:7).

So, what does this have to do with you and your dreams? This second temptation conveys many messages, but for the purposes of this reflection, consider these three:

The first is to remain humble. As St. Vincent de Paul said, "Good makes no noise; nor does noise do any good."[50] As your dreams become reality, remember, it isn't about you. You are, as the well-known prayer attributed to Francis of Assisi says, merely "an instrument of God's peace."

The second message is that you do not need to prove yourself to others. Jesus was challenged to reveal himself and his greatness; you may feel the same pressure. People, especially loved ones, may not understand your dreams. There will be doubters and naysayers. You will feel the need to make noise to help them understand. You may just want someone to believe in you. You may also operate out of the desire to prove someone wrong.

At a party launching his first publication, an author decided to list all the publishers that rejected previous manuscripts. This "I'll show you" mentality may feel satisfying in the moment, but it constrains us within a limited view of the world. Too bad that author didn't see those rejections as blessings, leading him to a publisher who shared his vision, and so producing a book that the world needed. Your dream must have God as its starting point and nothing else. Not starting from God's dream for you will lead only to disappointment and lack of fulfillment.

Another message within this second temptation is a reminder to trust in God. If what we perceive is truly God's dream, God is waiting for us to cooperate. That energy is ready to manifest itself, but our limitations hold us back. So, in this message comes a hope that only trusting in God can bring. It is a hope that will lead to action.

As an author I also have received my share of rejections. By allowing the time necessary for healing, I transitioned my negativity and disappointment to a place of peace and understanding, even when I did not truly understand the road ahead.

In this temptation Jesus is about to begin his ministry. He is about to go down a road of love and hate, of fame and of jealousy. Some will understand him, others not. What he does will be misinterpreted, even the cross, even his death and resurrection.

Jesus had to ponder these things in the desert. He knew the people he would be teaching well; he had lived among them for thirty years. He knew some would not understand, He also knew what had been prophesied. He could have gained superhero status had he plunged from the summit of the temple only to be saved. He chose a different way, a more authentic way. He did not test God. Neither should you.

Temptation #3: Power

The third temptation is power. The devil accompanies Jesus to the highest mountain peaks, overlooking many kingdoms. Jesus, who would be mocked at his death as "King of the Jews," is offered kingship if he worships this negative power. George Slatyer Barret interprets this temptation metaphorically, with Jesus being tempted to change his approach. Jesus was nonviolent and filled with love, but here he is tempted to fulfill his mission through power and political oppression. Barret writes, "[T]he old but ever new temptation to do evil that good may come; to justify the illegitimacy of the means by the greatness of the end."[51] Instead, Jesus chose a way of love that would lead to his death.

Jesus' temptation invites us to ask ourselves, is your dream worth dying?

The death may be literal, as it has been for some of our greatest, most inspirational leaders. It may be metaphorical, ending certain ways of our life to bring about greater focus and commitment. People may stop drinking or smoking to save their life, or to make better use of their time and money. People may seek forgiveness as they strive to achieve greater peace. A metaphorical death may require new sacrifices, giving up time and comfort in exchange for a greater good.

It is the sacrifice runners make every morning when they rise before the sun. It is the sacrifice of a teacher giving time to a failing student. It is the sacrifice that volunteers make on Saturday mornings to accompany the vulnerable—serving soup, providing clothes, offering a listening ear.

The devil offers Jesus the way of power, but he chooses the way of love. And that energy has swept through the generations for 2,000 years.

Over the centuries, in the name Christ many leaders fell to the temptation of power, engendering holy wars and abuse, domination and greed, and distrust. Others, however, emerged from the deserts of their life to walk as Jesus and other great spiritual teachers did, understanding that their dreams of the heart were truly the dreams of God. They may have never worn a crown, their name may never echo through time, but their love does, as it is a love like God's.

Following the third temptation, something spectacular happens. Miraculously, angels come to help and care for Jesus. God sends angels to us too, in the guise of our neighbors. At times, angels appear to lift our spirits, heal our wounds, and walk with us on the journey. We, in return, can serve as angels when we come to our neighbors' aid.

As you follow your heart and pursue your dreams, God sends you in service to your fellow pilgrims on this journey called life. It is a wonderful image, this angelic spirit of hospitality and care.

The temptations of the external world can always keep you from ministering to the world. The dream that stirs in your heart may well be the answer to someone else's prayer. You and I are called—indeed, required—to respond with love that comes from God.

Closing Thoughts

This chapter asks you to distinguish between the demands of society and God's dream for you. These first seven chapters have prepared you to identify the dreams you may have that can change the world. We now come to the point of finally dreaming. You are ready to take the next step to answer the call to bring God's dream, your dream, to life.

CHAPTER 8

TIME TO DREAM

The three activities that this chapter presents provide a template for identifying your dreams. Chapter 11 will offer a framework to bring one aspect of your dream to life. To prepare for that, this chapter provides a space to create and to dream big!

A few instructions before you begin.

First, remember the temptations mentioned in the last chapter. Remember also that the dreams you identify are of God—for the purpose of serving others. At the end of discerning these dreams, ask yourself a key question: will they matter after you die?

Second, do not limit your imagination. Too often people overthink these activities and get stuck by constraints such as money, time, or family situations. Chapter 10 will take these into consideration. For now, you are invited to dream without any limitation.

Third, pay attention to what brings you energy and what does not. If your dream weighs you down, throw it away. These dreams should bring a smile to your face, joy into your soul, and energy into your life. These dreams are of God, so take them seriously. Appreciate how the Spirit is moving through you in this process.

Activity 1: From 9 to 5

Disclaimer: This first activity invites creativity within a framework of a "typical" full-time 9am to 5pm job. This may not be your reality.

You may not be working at this time. You may work longer hours or share time between multiple jobs. You may be a student or are caring for loved ones, and your hours at work may be different than your "work" when you return home.

For this example, we will explore how to dream of a new work reality, but this is not intended to ignore or devalue your current reality.

Imagine if your 9 to 5 looked different.

If you are tired, frustrated, bored—could it be different? If you feel that you are not living to your full potential—not using your gifts and talents—can you, will you, change your life?

In this activity, you are invited to re-imagine your 9 to 5.

If you could do anything in the world as your "vocation," from 9am to 5pm, what would you do? (Do not take into account constraints or limitations such as paying bills, childcare, or time).

Allow this activity to stretch your imagination. If you come up with more than one idea, write them all down. There are no limitations.

Imagine a different world.

Example:

Meet Jane, a forty-year-old single mother of two. She currently works two jobs, takes care of her ailing mother, and is raising her ten-year-old and seven-year-old daughters. Her "job" is as a human resources representative at an office, but she has a side job creating t-shirt designs that she sells online.

In human resources, her exceptional listening skills benefit her company. She is also creative in problem-solving and finding solutions for difficult employee cases.

Jane's t-shirts provide what she calls "babysitting money." She gets about two dozen orders each month, often spending weeknights fulfilling the requests after feeding her children and getting them to bed. She finds joy in the creative process, even at eleven at night.

In this imagination activity, Jane dreams of owning her own design company. This side-job becomes her "9 to 5."

Jane imagines waking up in the morning, excited to head to a converted home-office space that used to be a storage room full of memories and mixed emotions. When she starts to clean that room, what in the past would have felt like an overwhelming task now brings her excitement and joy.

She first designs a layout, placing her desk so she could look out the window. She imagines the sun shining in the early hours as she is bringing new ideas to life. She imagines where to place a bookshelf, an easel in the opposite corner where her creative juices could flow.

As Jane boxes away items to donate and fills bags with things to dispose of, within her mind and her heart she sees her dream coming to life. Just cleaning her office is so exciting that she wants to stop this dream activity to start cleaning.

She then imagines what a day would like:

After getting the kids off to school, Jane returns to her quiet home. She pours herself a cup of coffee and heads into her space. She spends the first hour answering emails, reading and commenting on reviews, and returning phone calls.

She dedicates the next two hours to designing and creating, her favorite playlist in the background. Jane takes a lunch break, and then checks in on her mom, bringing her food and assuring herself that mom is taking her medicine.

On the way home, Jane stops at the post office to get out the day's shipment. She spends the afternoon printing invoices, packing the shirts, and preparing boxes for the next day's shipment. She imagines such a rhythm, which would leave her free each morning when she finds that she is most creative.

She imagines her designs becoming so popular that she needs to hire help to keep up with the orders. In time, she makes enough to invest in a small space to better handle production. Customer service is a priority, so she hires someone to take on that responsibility. She starts to make designs upon request, allowing for new creative challenges that allow her business to always stay fresh. She also has flexibility to attend after-school events with her children and to spend time with her mom. She makes up missed work at night and on the weekend.

In this dream process, Jane does not take into consideration the financial risks. She does not imagine the challenges that this career shift will bring, and how they may impact her life and her family. Jane knows that this dream may not turn out exactly as she envisions it, but the dream is leading her into a new reality.

Jane imagines that her new world will allow her to be a better mother, daughter, friend, and person. She knows that by following her dreams she will inspire others, especially her two daughters. Jane is also committed to giving back. She would commit to sustainable products that benefit the earth and the community. She is already purchasing fair-trade shirts for her small business to support her suppliers, whose labor is often taken advantage of.

Jane would also commit to donating a certain percentage of her profits to an organization that she values, and she would donate shirts for her children's local fundraising efforts. These is what Jane dreams of as she re-imagines her one, precious life.

The next chapter will follow Jane as she brings this dream to life.

Your turn:

In the space below, dream your 9 to 5. As we saw in Jane's example, be as detailed as possible and allow the dream to unfold. Enjoy this activity, as it may very well be the first step to a new, truer life.

Activity 2: Change the World—Take Two

In Part II, during the Discovery step, you reflected on five questions. The last was, "If you could change the world, how would you do it?"

This activity builds upon that question.

It asks how you might change the world today, this week, this month, and this year. Use this template for your responses.

Question	Idea	Action Plan
How will you change the world *today?*		
How will you change the world *this week?*		
How will you change the world *this month?*		
How will you change the world *this year?*		

You may find that your answers build upon one another, or you may find that you are answering each question with a quite different idea. Remember to use your gifts and talents to respond to these answers. Do not underestimate the importance even of something simple, like a generous gesture, helping a stranger in need, or reaching out to a distant, long-lost friend in changing the world. Changing the world also can be as big as you can imagine (such as human beings reaching the moon).

This activity invites creativity and generates a tentative timeline for bringing your dreams into reality. The example below demonstrates how it not only is possible, but exciting.

Example:

Ron is a sixty-year-old salesman. A recent job change now requires even more traveling and training. His experience benefits him and his new company, but he is growing tired with the work and competition. His children are in college and Ron is finding that he is missing something in his life. He is blessed with a marriage and family, but he is looking to making a greater impact than meeting his monthly quota.

Here is how Ron filled out the above activity:

Question	Idea	Action Plan
How will you change the world today?	Call distant cousin who suffered the loss of his wife a few months ago.	Call cousin after lunch.
How will you change the world this week?	Take on some of my family's house responsibilities so his spouse can take a day to refresh and refocus.	Schedule the responsibilities and time when I can complete them. Schedule a massage for my spouse at their favorite place and make a reservation for lunch at a local restaurant.
How will you change the world this month?	Provide a generous rate for a financially insecure elderly couple who are buying his product.	Need to seek approval from supervisor, calculate a fair deal for the couple and for the company.
How will you change the world this year?	Become a regular volunteer at church's food pantry.	Speak to leadership to assess need. Schedule the time I can commit and utilize my business skills to collect more food and to re-organize distribution.

Ron's last two dreams will require are key features of the Design step. This collection of information will allow Ron to make the dreams a reality.

You may be reading these dreams and thinking, "This isn't that difficult." Especially compared to the first activity, this activity feels more manageable. Like the first activity, it allows you to identify some of your gifts and talents as well as your passions. Ron uses his skills to benefit the couple in need but can also help hundreds at the food pantry. Note that he first plans to speak to leadership to assess the need. There may not be a need for increased collection of food or to re-organize distribution. He may use different skills to respond to different needs. He may be redirected to another need for the community.

Now that his children are more independent, he has identified a desire to help people in need on the weekends where he has time. Ron also identified two gestures, one for his cousin and one for his partner, that can make a difference in their lives. Like the "pay it forward" movement, his cousin and his partner may reach out to someone in their lives to offer a similar kind gesture.

I used this activity while teaching a doctoral course focused on higher education leadership. All the students were in higher education professional leadership positions. The directions were not limited to their job responsibilities but could be applied to their personal and professional aspirations.

Some students, like Ron, were more practical in their dreams. They imagined taking time to reach out to family and friends, or volunteering. Some considered how they could use their work to help the people they serve and work with, while others focused on improving their own spiritual life to prepare to help their brothers and sisters.

Others dreamed bigger. Some set more grandiose efforts as their month and year goals. One student said he would provide free college tuition for students in need.

One student dreamed of leaving her behind-the-scenes job in administration to become a teacher so as to connect with students directly. One student imagined adopting a baby, while another planned to move his parent in with him to provide better care.

The point of this activity is to focus your dreams and to start developing a plan. As mentioned before, the next part of this book will focus on designing and delivering your dreams.

Activity 3: Change the World–Take Three

Let's use the prior activity to examine one more example. It is different in that it responds directly to the needs of the world. You may find yourself feeling helpless, overwhelmed by the cry of the poor. This activity can be useful if you do not know what direction to take, or even where to start on such huge issues.

Let's take a social issue that is not only controversial, but difficult to resolve. For this activity, let's look at the issue of incarceration.

According to an American Civil Liberties Union (ACLU) report titled "Overcrowding and Overuse of Imprisonment in the United States," the US, which has only 5% of global population, has 25% of the world's prison population. Since 1970 the US prison population has increased sevenfold; 2.3 million people are incarcerated. The report continues, "Across the country, young Black men living in neighborhoods of concentrated disadvantage are disproportionately incarcerated and under correctional control. This phenomenon—the excessive use of incarceration and correctional control, especially among poor people and people of color—is commonly referred to as mass incarceration."[52]

This major problem has countless implications. These jarring statistics can and should make us ask, "How is this possible?" We can, and should, also ask, "Has anyone tried to remedy this injustice?"

The answer is that plenty are trying—many levels of the government, public and private institutions, grass roots movements in communities and families. The impact of stigma, subtle and explicit racism, and social and economic inequalities underlie this injustice, which is difficult to overcome. The good news is that despite the challenges, solutions are possible.

This is where you come in.

Your dreams may focus on being a part of a solution to mass incarceration, or a solution for another critical injustice in society.

For incarceration, your dreams may begin with gathering information on the crisis, including its history and the current state of affairs. You may sign up for updates from organizations like ACLU that are trying to help protect people's liberties. From this, your dreams may begin to emerge.

At the conclusion of this book, I share inspiring words from a commencement address given by Rev. Greg Boyle, S.J, founder of Homeboy Industries, Inc. He exemplifies someone who dreamed of a new response to incarceration, specifically incarceration related to gang violence.

He began his project in 1988, during a growing epidemic of young people killed in gang violence in Los Angeles. Homeboy Industries has become the largest gang intervention, rehabilitation, and re-entry program in the world. The dream started small, creating a social enterprise business to offer hope to the youth.

I strongly encourage you to read Boyle's *Tattoos on the Heart: The Power of Boundless Compassion* to learn more about how his dream changed the world.

Boyle dreamed of addressing gang violence and incarceration, and he has inspired countless others.

Allow your dreams to go beyond the walls of your home and the gates of your community.

Do not let your dreams be limited by other voices that echo outside and within.

Allow your dreams to respond to the cries of those being pushed further and further to the margins by power, greed, and status.

Allow God to dream through you.

Your turn:

Fill out the boxes below with four ways you can change the world. Remember, no dream is too small. Try to not get stuck on whether your dream is possible or not. The next step will move some of these ideas into action. What you may list as a dream for today may need a week or a month or more to bear fruit. Open yourself so that the Spirit can move you through this creative process.

Begin by identifying a societal injustice that weighs heavy on your heart.

Question	Idea	Action Plan
How will you change the world *today?*		
How will you change the world *this week?*		
How will you change the world *this month?*		
How will you change the world *this year?*		

Activity 4: Four Boxes

This activity is based on the work of Appreciative Education (The application of Appreciative Inquiry in the field of education).[53]

Its rationale is not only to identify your gifts and talents, but to map out a plan for your future.

By completing this activity, you will have a visual to keep you on target as you pursue this process.

This table will be your guide for this activity:

1. Adjectives/Description	2. Accomplishments
3. Award(s) you hope to receive	4. Drawing of self in ten years

1. Adjectives/Description:

In the first box, list adjectives or descriptive terms that you hope people will say about you six months from now. Although I have facilitated this activity with a dream for a year from now, or even five years, I recommend six months, as it is more realistic and holds you more accountable.

Examples could be adjectives or descriptions that already exist, or they could be something you are working on in your own holistic growth.

2. Accomplishments

In the second box, list your accomplishments for the next six months. This can be a list of dreams that you have for yourself. For example, they can be aspects of one dream (like writing parts of a novel or an autobiography), or many different accomplishments related to all aspects of your holistic growth.

3. Award(s) you hope to receive

In this third box, imagine how your dreams will be celebrated after they come to life. If you are working on your physical health, perhaps you will be profiled in a health magazine or have your photo posted on social media.

If you dream of ending poverty in your community, you may receive an award from a local society, organization, or government.

If you dream of writing a book, you may receive an award or find your book included on a recommended list.

If you dream of becoming a teacher, you may find yourself receiving an award in your district.

If you dream of adopting, you may receive a "dad of the year" card from your child.

Whatever your dream is, imagine how it can be celebrated. As you imagine this, dig deeper. Try to feel what it is like to be celebrated for your dream. Try to capture what this would be like. This activity is not meant to fill your ego. Rather, it is to help you realize how close you are to bringing this dream to life. It is within your reach.

4. Drawing of self in ten years

For some people, drawing releases a different creative process than writing does. This offers a challenge to imagine what your life will look like a decade from now. While the other questions have a shorter window, this box is intentionally "further away." This box may require significant changes. Your life might also be changed by welcoming new life, or by saying farewell to loved ones who return to God. While you can't predict this, you may take these factors into account for your future plans.

Students who have done this process with me produced drawings with common aspects. They often included families, which seem to represent what matters most. Other drawings included career and educational goals, travel plans, and new life accomplishments.

Do not worry about the quality of your drawings (stick figures are fine). Instead, let the Spirit use your hand to reveal what is in your heart.

Example:

Pam is a twenty-one-year-old college senior. About to graduate with a degree in psychology, Pam uses this activity to discern her future beyond the campus gates. In her own reflection and prayer, she feels a call to help youth and young adults with their mental health needs. When she participated in the Discover activities, she better recognized how God gave her exceptional gifts that would be sharpened with counseling skills and techniques. She is unsettled by the high suicide rates of at-risk youth and feels called by God to respond to this need.

Here is how Pam completes the first three boxes:

1. Adjectives/Description	2. Accomplishments
• Smart • Caring • Selfless • Patient Listener • Trusts my gut • Deep Faith • Compassionate • Loving • Trustworthy	• Work at a summer camp with at-risk youth. • Start graduate school in August. • Attend a young adult retreat with my place of worship. • Run three times a week to prepare for a 5k. • Write a message each day to a friend or loved one either by email, mail, text messages, or social media posts.
3. Award(s) you hope to receive	**4. Drawing of self in 10 years** *(While you would draw this, this is a description of what Pam drew)*
• Graduate with honors • Graduate degree • Best Counselor Award for therapists under 30. • Best Girl Friend card from partner. • Godmother for friend's child	• A woman sitting in an office talking with a person who is crying. • On her desk is a photo of her with her partner, children, and pet dog. • There is also a photo when she hiked a mountain. • On her wall are her diplomas and photos of family members. • On the counter she has a magazine where she is on the cover. • She has an icon of the Blessed Mother that she bought when she took a pilgrimage to Lourdes, France

Closing Thoughts

As these activities demonstrate, God has instilled many dreams within you to enhance your life and to change the world. They are rooted deep in your heart, right where God meets you every second of your being.

Remember these words from Pope Saint John XXIII:

> Consult not your fears, but your hopes and dreams. Think not about your frustrations, but about your unfulfilled potential. Concern yourself not with what you tried and failed in, but with what it is still possible for you to do.[54]

John XXIII, pope for less than five years, is best known for calling the Second Vatican Council, which rejuvenated the Catholic Church. Many of the changes made in this Council are taken for granted today. Before this Council, Mass was said in Latin, the role of laity in liturgies and leadership was limited, and the music and creativity that are now quite popular and welcomed would have been curtailed, if not prohibited.

He is also remembered as a Vatican diplomat who was vocal and active during the Holocaust, saving countless lives from concentration camps.

In December of 1963, exactly six months after his passing, he was posthumously awarded the Presidential Medal of Freedom, the United States' highest civilian award. The award's citation reads:

> His Holiness Pope John XXIII, dedicated servant of God. He brought to all citizens of the planet a heightened sense of the dignity of the individual, of the brotherhood of man, and of the common duty to build an environment of peace for all humankind.[55]

Consider this citation along with his words listed above. They are the bookends for your dreams.

As you approach living a renewed and fuller life, to paraphrase the Holy Father, remember to consult not your fears but your hopes and your dreams. Imagine all the unfulfilled potential that lives within you, and do not worry about where and when you have failed. Focus on what is possible. And when your life comes to an end, may the universe celebrate how you followed your dreams.

To paraphrase the citation, your life will lift the sense of dignity of all because of your example and your actions. Your care to change the world will build up peace and justice for all.

By using your gifts and talents, by identifying and following your dreams, may you finally listen and respond to God's specific call that is yours. It is time. Let's bring these dreams to life.

CHAPTER 9

RESPONSIBILITY

As I was writing this book, I was reminded of the connection and responsibility we have to one another. Allow me to begin this final chapter of Part II with a reminder of the urgency that you bring your dreams to life.

This chapter includes three stories. The first is about pigeons (yes, pigeons), the second about ancient and living doves, and the third about a student from Uganda.

The chapter concludes with a reflection on the call to holiness, the call to live for self and for others. It is a call to bring your dreams to life—if not for you, for those who need the gift that you will be for them!

The Pigeons

The first story occurred on my balcony in Queens, New York. I first noticed pigeons seeking refuge during a period of heavy weather in May.

It was a Monday night and we had rare tornado warnings, then an evening storm that was both magnificent and frightening. When I went on the balcony to check for damage after the storm, I noticed that pigeons were beginning to collect a small pile of branches. I immediately removed them, as it was dirty and unsanitary.

The next morning, while feeding our daughter, then twenty months old, we again noticed two pigeons on our balcony. I looked outside only to find an even larger collection of branches taking the shape of a nest. As I did the night before, I started to sweep them away. I noticed that about twenty feet away, from the roof of a neighboring house, the pigeons were watching intently.

As I continued sweeping, I could hear my daughter crying—not her typical tears of anger or hunger or disappointment at having to leave the park. Her emotion seemed to come from a deeper place.

I went inside, picked her up and brought her to the glass doors between our apartment and the balcony. I explained how birds can make nests anywhere, but it was not going to be here.

She stopped crying. She sensed in those pigeons something that I did not realize at that time. An egg was coming, and these birds had chosen our balcony as a safe space.

Later that night, I returned to find not only a nest, but in the middle of the twigs a small white egg. With my wife's encouragement and my daughter's help, we welcomed these pigeons into our fold. I understood that my daughter felt a deeper connection to them, and sensed they needed us.

If you grow up in New York City as I did, you know that, as George Costanza famously claimed in a 1997 episode of *Seinfeld*, we have "a deal" with pigeons. We coexist with them, as we do with squirrels. It wasn't as if we were accepting a family of beautiful robins or majestic hawks into our home. These were pigeons. Before this encounter I had never given them much of a thought.

Now, with an egg in our midst and feeling the connection our own baby had with this new chick about to be hatched, I was invested. That night my wife and I researched, learning that pigeons mate for life and that a second egg would soon arrive. Over the next few weeks the mother and father would rotate in sitting on the eggs, and after the chicks hatched a month of feeding and training would follow.

Over the next days and weeks, my daughter (and to an extent myself too) cared greatly for these birds. It was clear that she had a deep affection for them, a strong connection that at first I did not feel. Our experience speaks to two themes from this book: our connection to God's creation and our connection to God.

The first theme includes something more than our connection to our fellow human beings: our living connection to all in this world that is alive. Everything bears the design of the same Source. Perhaps you have noticed the deep connection between domestic animals and their caretakers, or of wild animals sensing an approaching storm—but this small encounter with pigeons was personal. Just like us, they were looking for a safe place to bring their babies into the world. We are connected more than we know. I strongly recommend Dr. Larry Dossey's book, *One Mind: How Individual Mind is Part of a Greater Consciousness and Why It Matters* for more insight into the connection between created beings that goes well beyond science and reason.

The second theme is own connection or disconnection from our God. As we get older, our sense of connection to God diminishes. As mentioned earlier, children can reveal reverence for all of God's creation. Adding to the growing list of "lessons I learned from my daughter," she taught me how to see and feel what these pigeons needed, even when I could not. How wonderful is it that we can all learn from one another, despite our age, experience, and species?

The Doves

My encounter with the pigeons reminds me of a "sermon" that Francis of Assisi gave to a tree full of birds. This holy man focused every second of his life on a mission to encounter God. He was so moved by God's spirit that he decided to tell the birds of God's great love for them. *The Little Flowers of St Francis* documents the sayings and miracles of this Italian mystic. It recounts Francis telling the birds:

> My little sisters the birds, ye owe much to
> God, your Creator, and ye ought to sing his
> praise at all times and in all places, because
> he has given you liberty to fly about into all
> places; and though ye neither spin nor sew,
> he has given you a twofold and a threefold
> clothing for yourselves and for your off-
> spring. Two of all your species he sent into
> the Ark with Noe that you might not be lost
> to the world; besides which, he feeds you,
> though ye neither sow nor reap. He has giv-
> en you fountains and rivers to quench your
> thirst, mountains and valleys in which to
> take refuge, and trees in which to build your
> nests; so that your Creator loves you much,
> having thus favoured you with such boun-
> ties. Beware, my little sisters, of the sin of
> ingratitude, and study always to give praise
> to God.[56]

The companions who witnessed this sermon noticed
the following: "As he said these words, all the birds began
to open their beaks, to stretch their necks, to spread their
wings and reverently to bow their heads to the ground, en-
deavoring by their motions and by their songs to manifest
their joy to St. Francis." [57] After Francis rejoiced with the
birds and blessed them, they flew away in all directions, to
spread the message of God's love to all parts of the world.

I often dismissed this story as another centuries-old, ex-
aggerated fable. After my own encounter with the pigeons,
however, I started to view this sermon differently. Not only
does it emphasize the value of our fellow creatures, but it
also reminds us to be grateful that God has provided so
much for us—not only to survive but to find joy in this life.

Isn't it appropriate, then, that Francis's love for the for-
gotten—the lepers cast out of society and the birds usually taken for granted—is represented by turtledoves that

always nest near a statue of St. Francis at the Basilica of St Mary of the Angels, a sacred space where St. Francis prayed often.

Anyone who has visited Assisi understands how this is possible. The spirit of this great man still lives there. He loved God, a love that led him to serve everyone, even the birds. Like the children who point us to the way of God, we can live our lives to glorify God—with our words, and with our actions.

To this point the book has invited you to perform an inner workup. This will prepare you for the next chapter, where you will bring your dreams to life.

The Student

Before we get to action steps, I conclude this chapter with a third and final story. In my role at the university, I often help students facing housing and food insecurity. Those who St. John's serves often have high financial need. A former colleague once referred to these students as "heroes," as they have to work multiple jobs, care for their families, succeed academically, and serve those most in need, all while growing and developing as young adults. I could not agree more.

At times, students do not have the housing security they need to be successful. Some live out of their cars; others move from couch to couch and from friend's home to friend's home. It is a heartbreaking reality.

In 2012, with an international student, I had one of the most difficult yet inspiring experiences in my pastoral ministry. To protect his identity, I will call him John. John was from Uganda, and he could afford college because a local community leader had promised to provide a scholarship for him. His mother spent the little money that she had to fly him from Uganda to New York.

I remember him for many reasons, but I clearly recall a small detail—he would not use my first name, as many other students do. He called me "Mr. Walters." It was his way of showing respect and gratitude. I have never felt that a title is necessary. I walk with students in their faith journey, and although there is always a natural power dynamic between teacher and students, it does not matter to me if they call me "Jimmy," or place "Mr." or "Dr." before my surname.

John and I met because he was running out of time. The scholarship from that community leader had not arrived, and it quickly became clear that it never would. He was the victim of a scam, and he faced a deadline to pay his tuition or lose his student status. Once he is no longer enrolled, an international student's visa becomes invalid. He either had to go home, or risk being arrested by Immigration and Customs Enforcement (ICE). When we met, he had two weeks left.

Over those two weeks I spent countless hours listening to John in person, and on the phone to his mother. I can still hear her desperate voice. She just wanted her son to attend college. The conversation changed from trying to find a solution to encouraging his return home. It was, still is, heartbreaking.

Eventually the university agreed to pay for a flight home but would not allow him to stay and study. I do not remember our last conversation, but I do remember his face as it changed from hope to despair. I could not help him. This remains one of my most difficult memories in ministry.

I bring up this student's story because of the harsh reality of dreams. Yes, God has dreams for all of us, but we do not all have the same opportunity to bring those dreams to life. Consider a 2017 Oxfam report that eight men possess the same wealth as the 3.6 billion who make up the poorest of humanity.[58]

It is not a fair or equal world.

Unfortunately, even though we can all dream of a better life, some will face greater obstacles than others.

Those eight extremely rich people can easily bring their dreams to life, as can many who may not have such wealth but have financially secure and healthy lives. For most people, this is not the case. Most Americans fortunate to have employment live paycheck to paycheck. Many individuals, both young and old, take care of loved ones. All people deal with the complexity of life and their own challenging issues, which may require psychological or medical help. Life is hard. Some people are buried in debt, others are lost in addiction or struggle with depression and anxiety or lack the physical or mental skills to progress in their professional and personal lives. Unequal access to education, healthcare, and work opportunities reflect our society's injustice.

Discrimination and bias can close opportunities and crush dreams. People may be treated differently or even persecuted because of their color, language, weight, age, disabilities, gender, or identity. Some have more privilege than others, and the "American dream" of "if you work hard enough, you can do whatever you want," is simply not true for all.

You may have encountered this reality in your life, perhaps most recently in your dreaming. You may find yourself snickering as you imagine a different reality. One can chase a dream, but at what expense? At what sacrifice, not just to self, but to the families that depend on them? These realities must be considered, and this book is not meant only for the most privileged who can afford to take chances.

If you do have more advantages, consider this reflection not as a personal attack but as an opportunity to support those for whom the field is not level. If you face greater disadvantages, do not allow these challenges to define you. Stay faithful to your dream, claim your voice and your rights, and despite all the past, present, and future challenges, even against all odds, continue to do your best.

My path to higher education might seem easier than many have followed, but it was built on the hard work of my parents, the mentorship of invested teachers and counselors, and the simple reality of my many privileges. My students remind me, show me, challenge me to be an advocate for them, to change structures of inequality, and to do all that I can to support their dreams.

Something More

As I was beginning to write this book Pope Francis issued the apostolic exhortation *Gaudete et Exsultate*, on achieving holiness in the modern world. The pope said the document is meant "to re-propose the call to holiness in a practical way for our own time, with all its risks, challenges, and opportunities."[59]

The pope's message confronts the difficult realities just mentioned head on. He provides this example:

> A woman goes shopping, she meets a neighbor and they begin to speak, and the gossip starts. But she says in her heart: "No, I will not speak badly of anyone." This is a step forward in holiness. Later, at home, one of her children wants to talk to her about his hopes and dreams, and even though she is tired, she sits down and listens with patience and love. That is another sacrifice that brings holiness. Later she experiences some anxiety, but recalling the love of the Virgin Mary, she takes her rosary and prays with faith. Yet another path of holiness. Later still, she goes out onto the street, encounters a poor person and stops to say a kind word to him. One more step.[60]

Expanding on the situation of meeting a homeless person on a cold night, the pope says: "I can view him or her as an annoyance . . . or I can respond with faith and charity and see in this person a human being with a dignity identical to my own."[61]

These are the dreams of God. Simple encounters. Do I see pigeons as an annoyance or as God's creatures who need refuge? Do I see immigrants fleeing war and inhumane situations as an annoyance or as God's children who need safety and love?

Pope Francis reminds us that we are connected, that we are called to holiness, or "whole"-iness. By living a life of service, we become whole. In an unequal world, we still dream, we live. Our actions, inspired by God, can change reality for ourselves and for others.

As you move into the design step of this process—strategizing God's dream for yourself—do so within your current reality. Every aspect of your dream may not be realistic, but some of it can be now, and perhaps, some later. You may not be able to quit a job to pursue a new career or may be unable to afford tuition for further classes. However, you may capitalize on your gifts and talents to take on a new project that brings you joy. It is not a matter of settling, but of making changes within your current reality

I am reminded of a story in one of Dr. Wayne Dyer's podcasts. He recounts going to do an interview at a radio station, but when he arrived the staff had just found out that the station changed formats and that they would be losing their jobs. People were devastated, but Dyer challenged them to pursue now what they could not pursue before. He invited them to bring their dreams to life. He predicted that a year later many of them would feel more fulfilled. What at first may have seemed a crushing blow could be an opening to be the truest form of themselves.

As you prepare to design your dreams, allow your perspective to change to see the possibilities, despite the challenges. Trust that God's Spirit is leading you to a path of holiness, rooted in love of God and love of neighbor.

Closing Thoughts

One of my favorite hymns is "The Summons" (1987), by John Bell and Graham Maule, a song based on the Gospel of Mark's depiction of Jesus calling the disciples. It exemplifies the vision of the Second Vatican Council.

These words capture our mission as God's creation:

Will you come and follow me if I but call
    your name?
Will you go where you don't know and
    never be the same?
Will you let my love be shown? Will you
    let my name be known,
will you let my life be grown in you and
    you in me?
Will you leave yourself behind if I but call
    your name?
Will you care for cruel and kind and never
    be the same?
Will you risk the hostile stare should your
    life attract or scare?
Will you let me answer prayer in you and
    you in me?
Will you let the blinded see if I but call
    your name?
Will you set the prisoners free and never
    be the same?
Will you kiss the leper clean and do such
    as this unseen, and admit to what I
    mean in you and you in me?
Will you love the "you" you hide if I but
    call your name?

Will you quell the fear inside and never be
the same?
Will you use the faith you've found to reshape the world around, through my
sight and touch and sound in you and
you in me?

Lord your summons echoes true when you
but call my name.
Let me turn and follow you and never be
the same.
In Your company I'll go where Your love
and footsteps show.
Thus I'll move and live and grow in you
and you in me.[62]

God is calling your name. God is moving you into a
new reality, one that will make you whole. Many of the
song's lines offer inspiration and challenge, but I am most
moved by these words: "Will you let me answer prayer in
you and you in me?"

God wants to use you to answer prayers.

Imagine that reality for a moment. It is like putting on
a pair of glasses and seeing the world with new clarity. God
can use you to answer others' prayers through your actions
and your dreams.

The size of your bank account or home does not matter. You may not have a dollar to your name, a job to go
to, or a minute to yourself. All of you, all of us, are called
to love. In this love, we are called to answer prayers. Your
dream is a prayer for God's creation.

It is now the time to answer some prayers.

PART IV

DESIGN

CHAPTER 10

DESIGN A NEW LIFE

Every January, first-year students who stop by my office have two familiar challenges. The first is heartbreak. Like clockwork, students who hoped to continue high school relationships as they transitioned into college find on returning home for winter break that because they have changed relationships have changed. This does not happen in every case, but it is a common narrative as I console and support students who are processing heartbreak and growth.

The other challenge for new college students is time management. After their first semester some are disappointed with their GPA; their transition proved more difficult than they anticipated. University studies are different than high school. You don't have class every day, but you have to keep up with significant reading and frequent papers. The challenge of managing schedules, responsibilities, and relationships leads to significant personal growth. Although my specialization is spirituality, I find myself not just providing new ideas for prayer and reflection but teaching time management skills.

This chapter is like such conversations. Your growth requires not only change and transition; it also requires reimagining how you spend your time.

Like Chapter 8, Chapter 10 offers three activities to transform your dream into a reality. Inspired by Appreciative Inquiry model, these activities incorporate the "Design" and "Deliver" steps.

Activity 1: Information Gathering

In an earlier chapter we reflected on the story of Jane, a single mother of two who dreamed of owning her own design company. She imagined what her day might look like under her new reality, even down to the design of her renovated home office.

While the dream was exciting, was it realistic? The biggest obstacle was her 9 to 5 job in human resources. There she used her gifts and talents well and received a particularly important paycheck.

Still, she desired more, and her side project had the potential to grow. She saw this dream as a way to live her true self.

The next step for Jane, and for you with your dreams, is to gather information. You have homework ahead. For Jane, this homework included looking into options that might allow her to pursue her dream.

If you were Jane, what options might there be for your next steps? List them below:

	Next Step Idea	Who to Contact
Option #1:		
Option #2:		
Option #3:		
Option #4:		

It is easier to do this activity when it is not about you. Use Jane as an example to expand your thoughts before you do this for yourself.

Here are some ideas that I generated for Jane. They may or may not resemble what you imagined.

	Next Step Idea	Who to Contact
Option #1:	Work part-time	Supervisor/Financial Planner
Option #2:	Work from home several days a week	Supervisor
Option #3:	Apply for new job with more flexibility	Financial Planner/ Career portals/ Career Coach
Option #4:	Quit job and work off of savings	Financial Planner/ Family

The final option is the most dramatic. It would require a change in lifestyle that may not be possible. Especially as a parent, if she receives family health insurance through her work this may not be an option. Even moving to a part-time role as in the first option may not be possible, as health insurance is often connected to full-time employment. However, there are possibilities, some of which Jane may not even realize—and that is what this activity explores.

The second option examines the possibilities of working from home. For some people, this may be a dream scenario. Jane could use the time normally required for travel to the office to expand her side business. With fewer in-person meetings, she could re-adjust her schedule to do more with her new efforts. For others, this idea may not be workable.

The third option also is a game-changer. The transition from a familiar job to a new one may require even more effort. She could, however, find a job that requires less time, or offers more flexibility. Rather than quitting her job, she may find one that pays more so she can invest more into her new company, which may remain a part-time effort.

Whatever Jane decides, she needs information. I list some of the people she might speak with who could inform her decision. If none of these options prove satisfactory, she will need to brainstorm other ideas.

Jane's goal is to expand her business to be able to create, and to live her best life. While such change requires time and energy and involves risk, consider the big picture. This is your one life. It is your one chance. At the end of your life do you want to be reciting your regrets, dying with your song still inside of you?

Several years ago, I taught a doctoral course in which students learned how to use the Appreciative Advising model in academic advising. In one exercise they were charged to facilitate the model with colleagues or students. One student used the Appreciative Inquiry techniques with two colleagues to support their professional growth.

This experience allowed her to learn much more about her colleagues. She described the experience as "learning how they tick." Behavior that before the exercise may have been confusing became clear as she asked reflective questions and listened.

When she walked them through this Design step, she heard her colleagues' challenges. They met the usual bumps, but it was not the end of the road. She shared the following: "What was most interesting was the excuses. They both had dreams, and realistic plans to implement to improve their professional and personal life. But their own issues of self-confidence and fear caused them to bring this process to a halt."

I raise this now as it reveals a common pitfall in the process—fear. It is easy to stay comfortable. Taking risks requires entering the unknown, and this can be scary.

With this in mind, let's briefly look at the notion of fear.

Swiss psychiatrist Elizabeth Kubler-Ross wrote *On Death and Dying* to explain the five stages of grief (denial, anger, bargaining, depression, and acceptance). She says this about fear:

There are only two emotions: love and fear. All positive emotions come from love, all negative emotions from fear. From love flows happiness, contentment, peace, and joy. From fear comes anger, hate, anxiety and guilt. It's true that there are only two primary emotions, love and fear. But it's more accurate to say that there is only love or fear, for we cannot feel these two emotions together, at exactly the same time. They're opposites. If we're in fear, we are not in a place of love. When we're in a place of love, we cannot be in a place of fear.[63]

When we fear, we are not operating out of love. If God is truly love, then you could say, "When we fear, we are not in a place of God." This is true. When we are in touch with God, there is nothing to fear.

In theory, this makes sense. In living, it is easier said than done.

As I was writing this book, I witnessed my daughter's growth and development. She teaches me lessons daily, including insights into fear. For example, by watching her I learned that when my wife and I are present, she does not fear.

When she is with us, she feels safe, so safe that she pushes boundaries. She knows no limitations. She feels no fear. When we are taken away, her behavior changes. Until she feels safe with the person watching her, she is more tentative and careful.

In this same spirit, we should feel safe because our loving God is watching over us. The God who gives us life is moving us to a way of being that is not constrained by fear but energized by love.

As you do this activity for yourself, be aware of the potential pitfall generated by fear, and remember God's love for you. In that frame of mind, replace Jane's dream with your own. List the names of individuals that you will need to consult.

Brainstorm all possibilities.

Complete the chart here, adding as many ideas as possible:

	Next Step Idea	Who to Contact
Option #1:		
Option #2:		
Option #3:		
Option #4:		

Once you identify an option, the next step is to contact the people who have the answers. This activity moves your dreams into action. Your inquiry may not require speaking to someone. Sometimes, an online search can provide clarity. However, from my experience (with apologies to my fellow introverts), speaking face to face allows for answers and understanding.

Question	Idea	Action Plan
How will you change the world today?	Call distant cousin who suffered the loss of his wife a few months ago.	Call cousin after lunch.
How will you change the world this week?	Take on some of my family's house responsibilities so my spouse can take a day to refresh and refocus.	Schedule the responsibilities and time when I can complete them. Schedule a massage for my spouse at our favorite place and make a reservation for lunch at a local restaurant.
How will you change the world this month?	Provide a generous rate for a financially insecure elderly couple who are buying my product.	Need to seek approval from supervisor, calculate a fair deal for the couple and for the company.
How will you change the world this year?	Become a regular volunteer at my place of worship's food pantry.	Speak to leadership to assess need. Schedule the time I can commit and utilize my business skills to collect more food and to re-organize distribution.

Activity #2: Change the World Part Two

Remember Ron, the middle-aged salesman who wanted more from his life? He was invited to complete this activity with the mandate to change the world (similar to what you completed in Activity #2 and #3 in Chapter 8). Here is how he responded:

This activity moves your dreams into a manageable and realistic action plan. The first two questions provide steps for today and this week. The next two, which ask how you will change your work this month and year, will require more time. Some dreams take longer but remember that every year is a compilation of months, which is a compilation of weeks, which is a compilation of days. The days add up, and although some dreams may need those many days, I promise you—it is worth it.

Revisit what you wrote or the second activity in Chapter 8, either referring to that table, or writing your new responses here:

Question	Idea	Action Plan
How will you change the world *today?*		
How will you change the world *this week?*		
How will you change the world *this month?*		
How will you change the world *this year?*		

This table *is* your to-do list.

Dedicate time each day to accomplish just one of your action-plan steps. You may have time to make a call only during a lunch break, or a few minutes to search online before you head to sleep.

How does it feel?

As you begin to gather information, listen to your gut. Pay attention to how you feel. As you gain information, you move a step closer to bringing this dream to life.

You may begin to feel fear in the pit of your stomach. It is understandable to feel this way as you are about to embark upon a more exciting and fulfilled life.

Are you anxious? This is also understandable, but if you are going to be anxious, shouldn't you be anxious about the unknown time limit on your life, and how you may never have another opportunity like the one right now?

Are you excited? You should be, as this energy that fills you is from God, moving you a step closer to fulfilling your dream.

Do you feel that you are too young? Remember what Jeremiah heard from God: "Do not say, 'I am only a boy;' for you shall go to all to whom I send you, and you shall speak whatever I command you" (Jer 1:7).

Do you feel that you are too old? Recall the inspiring words in Paulo Coelho's *The Alchemist* concerning a baker who always wanted to travel: [64] "People are capable, at any time in their lives, of doing what they dream of."

There is a wonderful line from Stevie Wonder's "There's a Place in the Sun": "'Cause there's a place in the sun where there's hope for everyone, where my poor restless heart's gotta run."[65]

I love the words, "my poor restless heart's gotta run." It is, as Wonder says, in a place "where there's hope for everyone." Your restless heart meets the hope of others. As Frederic Buechner famously wrote, "The place God calls you to is the place where your deep gladness and the world's deep hunger meet."[66]

Bring your dreams to life until your heart and soul are no longer restless, but at peace.

Wonder's song concludes: "There's a place in the sun and before my life is done, got to find my place in the sun."

Before your life is done, live in the sun, or as the theme of this book encourages, live a life of love that is of God.

Activity Three: 4 Boxes

The final activity in Chapter 8 invited you to complete these four boxes. Like the previous activity, either refer to what you wrote in that chapter or rewrite it here:

1. Adjectives/Description	2. Accomplishments
3. Award(s) hope to receive	4. Drawing of self in ten years

For whatever you wrote or drew, ask yourself this question: "How do I make this happen?"

For example, in box #1, what do you need to change to be described this way?

A word of caution. This isn't meant to focus on all your shortcomings and imperfections. That would leave you like a hamster on a wheel. We are human, after all. Instead, focus on something that you feel could be an area of growth.

You may want to be a better listener, so you may decide to read about counseling skills or take classes at a local college. You may want to be a better manager, so you can investigate workshops or webinars that focus on supervision skills. You may want to be more empathetic in relationships, which may lead to more volunteering or meditation. This task challenges you to look into the mirror and to search for what you have not yet noticed about yourself. As you search, remember to be gentle with yourself.

Box #2 lists the accomplishments that you hope to achieve by a to-be-determined date. If you are writing a book, list your deadlines for each chapter to be completed. There have been times that when I had a busy week ahead of me, so all I could accomplish was to write two pages, or to proofread earlier drafts. If you are focusing on your health, you may incorporate an online application to keep track of miles run, healthy eating habits, weight loss, or days at the gym. Some apps that celebrate milestones can encourage you along the way.

Box #3 lists the awards you hope to receive. If you are working on your health, you may picture receiving a medal as you cross the finish line. The next question is to map out how this can come to be in your life. It may start with running two minutes one day, slowly building your muscles and stamina. If you are dreaming of opening a new business, imagine awards in the form of positive reviews on websites or in newspaper columns. What will make your business unique and successful?

An example of this from my personal experience is Lieb Cellars, a winery on the North Fork of Long Island, New York. This emerging area contains more than sixty wineries, but Lieb stands out not only for its delicious wine, but also for its customer service. We make it out to the winery region a few times a year. Every time we go, we are treated like family. Known as "Team Lieb," the staff is knowledgeable, kind, and hospitable. Some wineries have a longer history and older vineyards, but this winery has managed to make its mark on Long Island by creating a sense of family. Consider this online review:

Whether you grab a seat inside Lieb Cellars' cozy tasting room, or make your way to the outside patio, your time will be full of fun and friendliness. The Lieb team is always on their feet to make visitors feel at home, with simple, yet educational information about their wines.[67]

Imagine if Lieb's general manager had set as a goal for the company to receive this positive review. The steps to follow would be not only to make great wine (which is no easy task), but to create a "fun and friendly" environment. The steps would have to focus on customer service and hospitality management. The staff would need training to speak knowledgeably to the diverse customers, while also understanding what each unique customer wants. This activity becomes the goal, and now you have to fill in the steps to achieve it.

Box #4 invites you to draw yourself in ten years; you may decide on a shorter timeline—perhaps a year, or five years. Your drawing reveals your goals.

One student in my first-year seminar drew herself in front of an orphanage. Surrounded by children, she was holding a diploma in one hand. In this drawing she identified her vocation as a doctor who serves this specific population of children. In the corner she also drew a guitar.

The images provide the goals. Her next step was to create a game plan for each goal. She was on her path to an undergraduate diploma. The academic road to a professional degree was long, but it started with her academic success right now. One of her next steps would be mapping future courses with her academic advisor, creating a timeline for next steps.

To serve abandoned children, she would need to learn more about this population. Where can she serve them and how? Are children in her local community or in another country? Would she need a medical degree, or might she use other gifts and talents? These are questions to consider, reflect on, and pray about, informed by what already exists and where gaps remain in service to children experiencing greater need and care.

At her side she drew a book that she had not yet started to write. She has ideas but would need to start writing to allow her creativity to flow. Other steps may include informing herself about the publication process and formats for books in the genre she intends to produce. She would also need to map out a writing plan, recognizing whether she plans the project now or in the future.

She also has a guitar, which, by the way, she does not own and does not know how to play. She may decide to take lessons, or to watch videos online. A student who played guitar at my daughter's christening amazed me. I complimented her talent and asked when she started playing.

To my astonishment, she had begun only three years earlier. She learned by watching YouTube clips after completing her homework.

This activity invites you to re-imagine your lives. Anything is possible. This statement is attributed to Thomas Edison, the inventor of the lightbulb: "If we did all the things we are really capable of doing, we would literally astound ourselves."

It is time for you to re-invent yourself. Your dream is your light bulb.

This chapter is a "how-to."

Edison invented the first practical incandescent lamp through exhausting research, along with trial and error. In the same fashion, this chapter invites you to do your research, to try and fail, and eventually, to try and succeed. From your hard, focused work, a light bulb will turn on. It will be in the form of a life well lived, and you will surely glow.

This can be said for spiritual leaders and those who live life at a higher energy level. They ooze love. Because they are faithful to their callings and vocations, they resonate light and life. They trust in something much larger than themselves, and they see their life as a ministry for others.

As this chapter concludes, I am reminded of an African proverb: "When the music changes, so does the dance."

My friends, the music is changing. Your life before was a different song.

This is a new chapter, and the music is changing. So, dance with a renewed spirit, knowing that your dance partner is God. Follow God's lead and take each step trusting in the music of a life of love. It is time to put your dancing shoes on.

CHAPTER 11

WHERE DOES IT HURT?

As I began writing this book, I heard about the social activist Ruby Sales, a legend in the civil rights movement. At age sixteen Sales participated in the 1965 marches from Selma to Montgomery. She was jailed for six days after picketing at a white-only store. After being released, she went to a nearby store with her friends, but they were shot at. One of her fellow marchers, Jonathan Daniels, pushed her away from the line of fire, only to be hit himself and killed.

Daniels, a nineteen-year-old Episcopalian seminarian, was valedictorian of his class. Sales was so traumatized that for seven months she could not speak. Despite death threats against her and her family, she testified at the trial of the alleged shooter, a special deputy named Tom Coleman. After an all-male, all-white jury found Coleman not guilty, Sales launched herself into a life of mission focused on justice.

Sales went on to attend the same seminary that Jonathan Daniels had attended, the Theological School in Cambridge, Massachusetts. She worked as a human rights activist in Washington DC, then founded a non-profit inner-city mission, The SpiritHouse Project, which she dedicated to Daniels.

Sales came to my attention because of a key question that she learned to ask during the civil rights movement: "Where does is hurt?" In a 2017 interview with Sales, Krista Tippet, host of the *On Being* podcast, said that asking where does it hurt "gets to the heart of the matter."[68] This question inspired Sugarland's 2018 country song, "Tuesday's Broken," composed in response to the all too common gun violence and suicide in America. The refrain is, "But what if we try to reach him in words, what if we looked into his eyes and asked, 'where does it hurt,' would he find all he was worth?"[69]

What if your dreams asked, "Where does it hurt?"

What if your dream then responded to the answer as you designed and delivered your plan?

This question is intended to lead you both inward and outward.

Where Does It Hurt You?

At times our biggest obstacle is our very self. The negative and limiting voices of the past echo in our mind and in our heart telling us what we should be, and what we should do with our life. Losses of loved ones, jobs, or status can shake us at the core, and sometimes we may never fully recover. The pain from bullying, violence, or trauma can endure for decades.

Many individuals remain stuck because their hurt that has never been cared for or mended—stuck in harmful relationships, inadequate employment, and circumstances that they cannot escape or move beyond. Some try to cope via substance abuse, others retreat, others burn bridges. Some abuse others, projecting their own hurt by lashing out against innocent victims, often those closest to them. Many are not even aware of their hurt and their hate.

If only they took the time to ask, "Where does it hurt?" If only someone else asked too. If only they found professional and medical support and the spiritual guidance to let the healing begin, then maybe they could live a life not constrained by the past.

Where Does It Hurt Others?

The "Where does it hurt" question is also external. The answer can guide our dreams. It can also be the answer to prayers.

Here is how Ruby Sales explained the origin of her question:

> A defining moment for me happened when I was getting my locks washed, and my locker's daughter came in one morning, and she had been hustling all night. And she had sores on her body, and she was just in a state, drugs. Something said to me, "Ask her, 'Where does it hurt?'" And I said, "Shelly, where does it hurt?" And just that simple question unleashed territory in her that she had never shared with her mother. And she talked about having been incested. She talked about all the things that had happened to her as a child, and she literally shared the source of her pain. And I realized, in that moment, listening to her and talking with her, that I needed a larger way to do this work, rather than a Marxist, materialist analysis of the human condition.[70]

This question changed Sales's life. It changed Shelly's life. Our lives change as this question gives us language and purpose. By asking others this question, we are moved to dedicate our time, our gifts, and our talents, to heal wounds.

One of my favorite scriptural passages speaks to this concept. In 1 Corinthians 12:12-26, St. Paul describes how "the body is one and has many members." Each part is critical, and a part of the same body. "If one member suffers, all suffer together with it; if one member is honored, all rejoice together with it" (1 Cor 12:26).

If this is true, as I believe it is, it reminds us of our responsibility to one another. It is in our interest for us to heal what is hurting in our human family. God instills these dreams in us with our neighbors in mind.

The challenge is in seeing the homeless on the street, the refugee, the person addicted to drugs and alcohol, all people on the margins as our responsibility to support to heal. Do you not feel the same responsibility to have your foot fixed if it is broken, or your back if it is not aligned? You must heal it so you can continue living. Imagine if we looked as one another with this same mindset.

A self-serving dream is not God's dream. The dream worth pursuing, the dream worth living, is a dream for all people. It is this dream that will bring you true joy. As St. Ignatius Loyola is reported to have said, "Whatever you are doing, that which makes you feel the most alive, that is where God is." Likewise, according to Rumi, "Love is the bridge between you and everything."

As you bring your dreams to life by delivering the designs from the previous chapter, look critically at your purpose. Does it respond to the hurt in this world? Does it seek justice amid injustice? Does it move us closer to equality and peace?

Together, let's fulfill the words of Jesus in his desire that we become one.

CONCLUSION

Consider this final chapter as a kind of commencement address. In a graduation ceremony, you look back on the time and emotional and physical energy you have invested in your life. By following the steps in the previous chapters inspired by Appreciative Inquiry, you have participated in activities and reflection that now allow you to make changes in your life.

Like a graduate, it is time to put all that you learned about yourself and the needs of the world into action. As you ask, "Where does it hurt?" you learn the needs not only of your soul, but also of those pilgrims who share this earthly journey.

Graduation Day

For over a decade, every May I worked graduation at St. John's University. I was often behind the scenes while over two thousand names were called during the three-hour ceremony. One by one, the graduates would cross the stage, receive a rolled-up piece of paper, and shake the hand of their dean.

Their families cheered, reflecting on the sacrifice many had made for this achievement. For the graduate, this chapter of life, their college career, came to a close. Some would remain or attend other campuses for further education. Some would enter a new career, others would commit to a year of service, and yet others would search for what is next in the subsequent chapters of their lives.

This preparation happened in and out of the classroom. They not only received a credential, but they gained experiences that formed them for what would happen next. Working at a mission-based and faith-based university, we hoped they cared about and had love for the poor, felt the responsibility to live their lives in service to others. As Rev. Greg Boyle, the founder of Homeboy Industries said at Whittier College's 2014 commencement, "It would not surprise us that God's own dream for us—that we be one— just happens to be our deepest longing for ourselves."[71]

He added, "For it turns out, it's mutual."

In that same spirit, remember that God's dream for you is not just for you. Your dream will answer prayers. The only question left is, will you?

Will you answer prayers by pursuing dreams?

Will you enter what Joseph Campbell called the "hero's journey" to a time of self-discovery and change?

Will you live God's dream?

You can close this book and think differently. You may even get as far as completing the activities in the earlier chapters. And even if you manage to do only that, then we must trust that God will continue to meet you where you are to move you further down the road. Or you can make the next step in your life right now. Your dreams, God's dreams, can come true.

Bronnie Ware, a palliative care nurse from Australia, wrote *The Top Five Regrets of Dying*, This is the top regret that she heard while caring for people in their last days:

> "I wish I'd had the courage to live a life true to myself, not the life others expected of me.". . . This was the most common regret of all. When people realize that their life is almost over and look back clearly on it, it

is easy to see how many dreams have gone unfulfilled. Most people had not honored even a half of their dreams and had to die knowing that it was due to choices that they had made, or not made. Health brings a freedom very few realize, until they no longer have it.[72]

So, what will it be?

Before you take your last breath, will you look back at your life and smile as you chased your dreams or, like so many others, will you be wondering "What if?"

Movement

The word "movement" invokes a collective energy. Movements are never individual. They unite efforts, built on support, understanding, and action. Take for example the Focolare Movement, founded by Chiara Lubich. It has evolved to respond to the needs of the world while remaining faithful to the goal of unity. I pray that this book supports the larger Focolare Movement, as well as the countless other movements rooted in justice, peace, and love.

I was invited recently to participate in a task force for the International Vincentian community. Our goal was to find a more productive way to communicate the Vincentian charism to a larger, younger audience. One of the leaders focused on the word "movement." The Vincentian community began as a movement. Its founder, St. Vincent de Paul, built communities to care for the poor, create new systems that were just, and lift the spiritual awareness of everyone they encountered. This engendered a global movement that has continued for four hundred years.

I like to think of this book as a movement, too. The focus on recognizing God's dream for you and then moving into action is similar to what Chiara began in 1943, and Vincent in 1617. They came to understand God's dream for them because they heard an inner call and responded with love. In their footsteps, those who follow them (and Jesus) are changing the world.

Ruby Sales, Greg Boyle, Chiara Lubich, Vincent de Paul, and many others identified in this book started or joined movements to respond with love to a hurting world. We too are invited to respond to God's unique call for us. We are all called to encounter God in the depth of our dreams and in our encounters with one another, especially those most in need. We must use our unique gifts to join others in reflecting the love of our God. This book invites you to move into action, to change the world as only you can.

The conclusion of this final chapter encourages collaboration and support within this journey of identifying and living the dream God has for each one of us. This can only come from recognizing God's presence in our life—which requires time each day in relationship with God. When a Daughter of Charity asked, "What should I do when I am praying but a person in need comes knocking at my door?". Vincent de Paul responded, "Go from God to God."

This example captures the balance of contemplation and action. In Christian scripture, it would be the story of Martha and Mary. One ministers to Jesus, while the other sits and listens. We are called to do both, to experience God in silence and in service. In these interactions God meets us and we meet God. God is always knocking at the door of our heart. We just need to answer.

As you own your place in this movement, I encourage you to share your experiences with one another. By using the hashtag #DreamsComeTrue on social media, let us share how we are using our gifts and talents in a life well lived. When you feel down and out, search this hashtag and be inspired. When you are living your best life, add your experience to #DreamsComeTrue so you can inspire others. Together, we can join existing movements and make our own movement that can change the world.

EPILOGUE

I like Broadway. I enjoy a night at a show, getting lost in a story and being inspired by amazing talent.

One of the more famous shows that has entertained generations is *Les Misérables*, based on the book by Victor Hugo. Its final scene shows the death of the main character, Jean Valjean. Earlier Valjean is shown mercy by Bishop Myriel after he attempts to steal from the church. Myriel's mercy launches Valjean down a different life path, a path of love. Some believe that Myriel's character is based on Vincent de Paul, the saint and priest that I have mentioned often in this book.

A song in *Les Misérables*, "Epilogue," includes the well-known refrain, "To love another person is to see the face of God." I humbly begin the "Epilogue" of this book with that same message.

To love another person is to see the face of God.

This book is one of my dreams. The steps inspired by Appreciative Inquiry guided me in bringing it to fruition. Time in prayer and reflection allowed me to see broken roads turn into streets of gold, leading me down this path at the right time.

For so long, when people would ask what is next in my professional life I would respond, "I feel like I have a book in me." And not just any book, but a love letter and a plea from God to us. As these pages unfolded, I was humbled as the book wrote itself. Thoughts would emerge from inspiration that I did not anticipate. I didn't worry as I did before about getting published. I didn't worry what people would think. I knew this to be my mission, my partnership in a shared dream that God planted within.

As I conclude, I pray that this book moves you closer to God. I pray it moves you closer to selfless action, focused on those on the margins. I pray that you truly live.

The world is waiting.

God is waiting.

We need you to be you.

And remember that your dreams, God's dreams, can and will come true.

NOTES

1. Tertullian et al., *Apology: De Spectaculis* (London: W. Heinemann, 1953)) 39, 7.

2. Martin Luther King Jr., "What is Your Life's Blueprint?" (speech, Philadelphia, PA, October 26, 1967), https://www.drmartinlutherkingjr.com/whatisyourlifesblueprint.htm.

3. "Remembering Spiritual Masters: Henri Nouwen," *Spirituality and Practice*, https://www.spiritualityandpractice.com/explorations/teachers/henri-j-m-nouwen/quotes.

4. "Isocrates, Nicocles or the Cyprians," George Norlin, Ed., *Isocrates, Nicocles or the Cyprians*, section 61, http://www.perseus.tufts.edu/hopper/text?doc=Perseus:text:1999.01.0144:-speech=3:section=61.

5. Jacob Neusner, *The Golden Rule: The Ethics of Reciprocity in World Religions* (London: Continuum, 2009),103.

6. William Woodville Rockhill, *Udânavarga: A Collection of Verses from the Buddhist Canon* (London: Routledge, 2000), 5:18.

7. Cited in Michael Hansbury, *The Problem behind All Problems* (New Delhi: Epitome Books, 2009), 128.

8. Cited in Harry J. Gensler, *Ethics and the Golden Rule* (London: Routledge, 2013), 55.

9. Cited in Heiner Roetz. *Confucian Ethics of the Axial Age: a Reconstruction under the Aspect of the Breakthrough toward Postconventional Thinking* (Albany: State University of New York Press, 1993), 136.

10. David L Cooperrider and Diana Whitney. *Appreciative Inquiry: A Positive Revolution in Change* (California: Berrett-Koehler Publishers, 2005).

11. Cited in John Chirban, "Seven Qualities of the True Self," *Psychology Today*. https://www.psychologytoday.com/us/blog/alive-inside/201304/seven-qualities-the-true-self.

12. Richard Rohr, "You are the 'Imago Dei,'" *Center for Action and Contemplation* (31 July 2016), https://cac.org/you-are-the-imago-dei-2016-07-31/.

13. Thomas Merton, *New Seeds of Contemplation* (New York: New Directions, 1972), 37.

14. Cited in Matt Emerson, "Merton and the 'True Self," *America* (22 November 2013), https://www.americamagazine.org/faith/2013/11/22/merton-and-true-self.

15. Marianne Williamson, *A Return to Love: Reflections on the Principles of A Course in Miracles* (New York: HarperCollins, 1992), 165.

16. Wayne Dyer, "The Power of I Am," https://www.drwaynedyer.com/blog/the-power-of-i-am/.

17. Cited in "20 Quotes from the Ancient Scriptures of Hinduism," *Become an Ordained Interfaith Chaplain or Community Minister* (9 August 2018), https://chaplaincyinstitute.org/portfolio-items/20-quotes-from-the-ancient-scriptures-of-hinduism/.

18. Jim Manney, "The Examen—the Prayer That Changes Everything," *Our Sunday Visitor* (24 January 2019), https://www.osvnews.com/2011/03/23/the-examen-the-prayer-that-changes-everything/.

19. Rūmī Jalāl al-Dīn et al., *Rumi, Selected Poems* (London: The Folio Society, 2017), 109.

20. Cited in Gary D. Chapman, *Love Is a Verb* (Minneapolis: Bethany House Publishers, 2009), 3.

21. Henri J. M. Nouwen, *Only Necessary Thing: Living a Prayerful Life* (New York: Crossroad, 2008),40.

22. Enzo Lodi, *Saints of the Roman Calendar: Including Recent Feasts Proper to the English-Speaking World* (Lulu.com, 2018), 47.

23. Katja Valli, Robert J. Hoss and Robert P. Gongloff, *Dreams Understanding Biology, Psychology, and Culture* (Santa Barbara, CA: Greenwood, an imprint of ABC-CLIO LLC, 2019), 439.

24. Henri J.M. Nouwen, *Return of the Prodigal Son: Story of Home-coming* (New York, Doubleday, Reissue Edition, 1994), 20.

25. Johannes Eckhart, *Meister Eckhart's Sermons*, Sermon IV, "True Hearing," http://www.ccel.org/ccel/eckhart/sermons.vii.html.

26. Bryan N. Massingale, "Welcoming the Stranger" (Speech, Queens, New York, 9 January 2018).

27. Jim Wallis, "Arrested in Ferguson in an Act of Repentance," *HuffPost* (15 December 2014), https://www.huffpost.com/entry/arrested-in-ferguson-in-a_b_5989346.

28. "Remembering Spiritual Masters: Henri Nouwen," *Spirituality and Practice*, https://www.spiritualityandpractice.com/explorations/teachers/henri-j-m-nouwen/quotes.

29. G.K. Chesterton, *Collected Works* (San Francisco: Ignatius Press, 1986), 29.

30. Cited in Victor A. Copan, *Changing Your Mind: The Bible, the Brain, and Spiritual Growth* (Eugene, OR: Cascade Books, 2016), 214.

31. Copan, 215.

32. Massingale.

33. Cited in Eddie Gibbs, *Leadership Next: Changing Leaders in a Changing Culture* (Downers Grove: InterVarsity Press, 2005), 185.

34. Martin Luther King Jr., "I've Been to the Mountain Top" (speech, Memphis TN, 3 April 1968), https://www.americanrhetoric.com/speeches/mlkivebeentothemountaintop.htm

35. King, "I've Been to the Mountain Top."

36. Cited in Vera M. Kutzinski, *The Worlds of Langston Hughes: Modernism and Translation in the Americas* (Ithaca: Cornell U Press, 2013), 131.

37. Annemarie Schimmel, *Triumphal Sun: a Study of the Works of Jalāloddin Rumi* (Albany: State University of New York Press, 1993), 289.

38. Schimmel, 289-290.

39. Lawrence Kohlberg, Sohan Modgil, and Celia Modgil, *Lawrence Kohlberg: Consensus and Controversy* (New York: Routledge, 2011), 24.

40. Teresa de Calcutta, Jaya Chaliha, and Edward Le Joly, *The Joy in Loving: A Guide to Daily Living* (New York: Arkana, 2000), July 12.

41. Martin Luther King Jr., "What is Your Life's Blueprint?" (speech, Philadelphia, PA, 26 October 1967), https://www.drmartinlutherkingjr.com/whatisyourlifesblueprint.htm.

42. Parker J. Palmer, *Let Your Life Speak: Listening for The Voice of Vocation* (San Francisco: John Wiley and Sons Inc., 2000), 4-5.

43. Palmer, 10.

44. Chiara Lubich at the 1977 Eucharistic Congress, Pescara, Italy, https://www.focolare.org/en/chiara-lubich/chi-e-chiara/.

45. Henri J. M. Nouwen and Sue Mosteller, *Home Tonight: Further Reflections on the Parable of the Prodigal Son* (London: Darton, Longman Todd, 2009), 38.

46. Cited in "20 Quotes from the Ancient Scriptures of Hinduism," 4.

47. "Happy Ending," https://www.lyrics.com/lyric/9807352/Sugarland/Happy Ending.

48. Henri J. M. Nouwen and Gerard W Hughes, *Reaching Out: a Special Edition of the Spiritual Classic, Including "Beyond the Mirror"* (London: Fount, 1998), xvi.

49. Thomas Merton, *No Man Is an Island* (Boston: Shambhala, 2005), 132.

50. Charles L. Souvay, "The Society of St. Vincent de Paul as an Agency of Reconstruction," *The Catholic Historical Review*, 7, no. 4 (1922), 446.

51. George S. Barrett, *The Temptation of Christ* (New York: Macmillan, 1883), 150.

52. American Civil Liberties Union (ACLU), *Overcrowding and Overuse of Imprisonment in the United States*, submission to the Office of High Commissioner for Human Rights (May 2015), https://www.ohchr.org/Documents/Issues/RuleOfLaw/Over-Incarceration/ACLU.pdf.

53. Jennifer L. Bloom, Bryant L. Hutson, and Ye He, *The Appreciative Advising Revolution* (Champaign, IL: Stipes Pub., 2008).

54. Eric Garner, *The Art of Personal Effectiveness: 500 Quotes on Making the Most of Yourself* (Bookboon.com, 2012), 18.

55. *Public Papers of the Presidents of the United States. John F. Kennedy: Containing the Public Messages, Speeches, and Statements of the President, January 1 to November 22, 1963* (Washington DC: U.S. Government Printing Office, 1964), 903.

56. Brother Ugolino, *The Little Flowers of St. Francis* (Grand Rapids: Christian Classics Ethereal Library, 1930), 38.

57. Ugolino.

58. "Just 8 Men Own Same Wealth as Half the World," *Oxfam International* (1 March 2018), https://www.oxfam.org/en/press-releases/just-8-men-own-same-wealth-half-world.

59. Francis, *Gaudete et Exsultate*, 5,2, vatican.va/content/francesco/en/apost_exhortations/documents/papa-francesco_esortazione-ap_20180319_gaudete-et-exsultate.html.

60. Francis 1,2

61. Francis.

62. John L. Bell, Graham Maule, and Iona Community, "The Summons," Hymnary.org, https://hymnary.org/text/will_you_come_and_follow_me.

63. Elisabeth Kübler-Ross, and David Kessler, *Life Lessons: Two Experts on Death & Dying Teach Us about the Mysteries of Life & Living* (New York: Scribner, 2014), 118.

64. Paulo Coelho, *The Alchemist* (New York: HarperCollins Publishers, 1998), 23.

65. "A Place in the Sun," https://www.lyrics.com/lyric/573314/Stevie Wonder/A Place in the Sun.

66. Frederick Buechner, *Wishful Thinking: A Theological ABC* (London: Collins, 1973), 95.

67. Melissa Kay, "5 Must-Visit Long Island Wineries for Any Wine Lover," *The Journiest* (12 December 2017), https://www.journiest.com/long-island-ny-wine-tasting-2516416431.html.

68. Krista Tippet and Ruby Sales, "Where Does it Hurt," 17 August 2017, in *On Being with Krista Tippett*, podcast, MP3 audio, 51:59, https://onbeing.org/programs/ruby-sales-where-does-it-hurt-aug2017/.

69. "Tuesday's Broken," https://www.lyrics.com/lyric/35019782/Sugarland/Tuesday's Broken.

70. Tippet and Sales.

71. Greg Boyle, "Commencement Keynote" (speech, Whittier CA, 16 May 2014), https://www.whittier.edu/news/fri-05232014-316-pm/father-gregory-j-boyle-2014-commencement-keynote-speech.

72. Bronnie Ware, "Bronnie Ware," (blog), https://bronnieware.com/blog/regrets-of-the-dying/.

WORKS CITED

"A Place in the Sun." A Place in the Sun Lyrics. https://www.lyrics.com/lyric/573314/Stevie Wonder/A Place in the Sun.

American Civil Liberties Union (ACLU). *Overcrowding and Overuse of Imprisonment in the United States*, Submission to the Office of High Commissioner for Human Rights, May 2015. https://www.ohchr.org/Documents/Issues/RuleOfLaw/OverIncarceration/ACLU.pdf.

Barrett, George S. *The Temptation of Christ*. New York: Macmillan, 1883.

Bell, John L., Graham Maule, and Iona Community. "The Summons." Hymnary.org. https://hymnary.org/text/will_you_come_and_follow_me.

Bloom, Jennifer L., Bryant L. Hutson, and Ye He. *The Appreciative Advising Revolution*. Champaign, IL: Stipes Pub., 2008.

Boyle, Greg. "Commencement Keynote." Whittier College, May 16, 2014. https://www.whittier.edu/news/fri-05232014-316-pm/father-gregory-j-boyle-2014-commencement-keynote-speech.

Buechner, Frederick. *Wishful Thinking: a Theological ABC*. London: Collins, 1973.

Calcutta, Teresa de, Jaya Chaliha, and Edward Le Joly. *The Joy in Loving: a Guide to Daily Living*. New York: Arkana, 2000.

Campbell, Joseph. *The Hero with a Thousand Faces*. Princeton: Princeton University Press, 1972.

Chapman, Gary D. *Love Is a Verb*. Minneapolis: Bethany House Publishers, 2009.

Chesterton, GK. *Collected Works*. San Francisco: Ignatius Press, 1986.

Chirban, John. "Seven Qualities of the True Self," *Psychology Today*. [Online]. https://www.psychologytoday.com/us/blog/alive-inside/201304/seven-qualities-the-true-self.

Coelho, Paulo. *The Alchemist*. New York: HarperCollins Publishers, 1998.

Cooperrider, David L., and Diana Whitney. *Appreciative Inquiry: A Positive Revolution in Change.*California: Berrett-Koehler Publishers, 2005.

Copan, Victor A. *Changing Your Mind: The Bible, the Brain, and Spiritual Growth*. Eugene OR: Cascade Books, 2016.

Dyer, Wayne. *"The Power of I Am,"* Drwaynedyer.com, accessed June 1, 2019, https://www.drwaynedyer.com/blog/the-power-of-i-am/.

Eckhart, Johannes. *Meister Eckhart's Sermons*, Sermon IV, "True Hearing," http://www.ccel.org/ccel/eckhart/sermons.vii.html,accessed June 1, 2019.

"Isocrates, Nicocles or the Cyprians." George Norlin, editor. *Isocrates, Nicocles or the Cyprians*, section 61. http://www.perseus.tufts.edu/hopper/text?doc=Perseus:text:1999.01.0144:speech=3:section=61.Ji.

Francis. *Gaudete et Exsulate*. vatican.va/content/francesco/
en/apost_exhortations/documents/papa-francesco_
esortazione-ap_20180319_gaudete-et-exsultate.
html.

Garner, Eric, *The Art of Personal Effectiveness: 500 Quotes on
Making the Most of Yourself*. Bookboon.com, 2012.

Gensler, Harry J. *Ethics and the Golden Rule*. London: Routledge, 2013.

Gibbs, Eddie. *LeadershipNext Changing Leaders in a Changing Culture*. Downers Grove, IL: InterVarsity Press,
2005.

Hansbury, Michael. *The Problem behind All Problems*. New
Delhi: Epitome Books, 2009.

"Happy Ending." Happy Ending Lyrics. https://www.lyr-
ics.com/lyric/9807352/Sugarland/Happy Ending.

"Just 8 Men Own Same Wealth as Half the World." *Oxfam International*, March 1, 2018. https://www.ox-
fam.org/en/press-releases/just-8-men-own-same-
wealth-half-world.

Kay, Melissa. "5 Must-Visit Long Island Wineries for Any
Wine Lover." *The Journiest*. July 1, 2019. https://
www.journiest.com/long-island-ny-wine-tast-
ing-2516416431.html.

King Jr., Martin Luther. "I've Been to the Mountain Top."
Address delivered at Mason Temple. https://www.
americanrhetoric.com/speeches/mlkivebeentothe-
mountaintop.htm

King Jr., Martin Luther. "What is Your Life's Blueprint?"
Address delivered at Barratt Junior High School.
https://kinginstitute.stanford.edu/king-papers/
documents/lifes-blueprint.

Kübler-Ross, Elisabeth and David Kessler. *Life Lessons: Two Experts on Death & Dying Teach Us about the Mysteries of Life & Living.* New York: Scribner, 2014.

Kutzinski, Vera M. *The Worlds of Langston Hughes: Modernism and Translation in the Americas.* Ithaca: Cornell Univ. Press, 2013.

Lodi, Enzo. *Saints of the Roman Calendar: Including Recent Feasts Proper to the English-Speaking World.* Lulu. com, 2018.

Lubich, Chiara. "1977 Eucharistic Congress," Pescara, Italy, https://www.focolare.org/en/chiara-lubich/chi-e-chiara/

Manney, Jim. "The Examen—The Prayer That Changes Everything." *Our Sunday Visitor*, January 24, 2019. https://www.osvnews.com/2011/03/23/the-examen-the-prayer-that-changes-everything/.

Massingale, Bryan N., "Welcoming the Stranger." Speech, Queens, New York, January 9, 2018.

Merton, Thomas. *No Man Is an Island.* Boston: Shambhala, 2005.

Neusner, Jacob. *The Golden Rule: the Ethics of Reciprocity in World Religions.* London: Continuum, 2009.

Nouwen, Henri J.M. *Bread for the Journey: A Daybook of Wisdom and Faith.* New York: HarperOne Reprint edition, 2006.

Nouwen, Henri J. M. *Only Necessary Thing: Living a Prayerful Life.* New York: Crossroad, 2008.

Nouwen, Henri J.M. *Out of Solitude: Three Meditations on the Christian Life.* Notre Dame, IN: Ave Maria Press, 1974.

Nouwen, Henri J. M. and Gerard W Hughes. *Reaching out: A Special Edition of the Spiritual Classic: Including "Beyond the Mirror."* London: Fount, 1998.

Nouwen, Henri J.M. *Reaching Out: The Three Movements of the Spiritual Life.* New York: Doubleday, 1975.

Nouwen, Henri J. M. *Return of the Prodigal Son: Story of Homecoming.* New York: Doubleday, Reissue Edition, 1994.

Palmer, Parker J. *Let Your Life Speak: Listening for The Voice of Vocation.* San Francisco: John Wiley and Sons Inc., 2000.

Public Papers of the Presidents of the United States. John F. Kennedy: Containing the Public Messages, Speeches, and Statements of the President, January 1 to November 22, 1963. Washington: U.S. Government Printing Office, 1964.

"Remembering Spiritual Masters: Henri Nouwen." *Spirituality and Practice.* https://www.spiritualityandpractice.com/explorations/teachers/henri-j-m-nouwen/quotes.

Rockhill, William Woodville. *Udânavarga: A Collection of Verses from the Buddhist Canon.* London: Routledge, 2000.

Roetz, Heiner. *Confucian Ethics of the Axial Age: A Reconstruction under the Aspect of the Breakthrough toward Postconventional Thinking.* Albany, NY: State University of New York Press, 1993.

Rohr, Richard. "You are the 'Imago Dei,'" *Center for Action and Contemplation,* 31 July 2016. https://cac.org/you-are-the-imago-dei-2016-07-31/

Rūmī Jalāl al-Dīn, Coleman Barks, Michael Schmidt, and Marian Bantjes. *Rumi, Selected Poems.* London: The Folio Society, 2017.

Sanders, J. Oswald. *Spiritual Leadership: Principles of Excellence for Every Believer.* Chicago: Moody Publishers, 2007.

Schimmel, Annemarie. *Triumphal Sun: A Study of the Works of Jalāloddin Rumi.* Albany: State University of New York Press, 1993.

Souvay, Charles L. "The Society of St. Vincent de Paul as an Agency of Reconstruction." *The Catholic Historical Review* 7, no. 4 (1922), 446.

Tippet, Krista and Ruby Sales. "Where Does it Hurt," August 17, 2017, *On Being with Krista Tippett*, podcast, MP3 audio, 51:59. https://onbeing.org/programs/ruby-sales-where-does-it-hurt-aug2017/.

Tertullian, *Apolog*ia: *De Spectaculis.* London: Harvard University Press,1953.

"The Inner Life of Social Change—Ruby Sales: Becoming Wise." *The On Being Project,* June 17, 2019. https://onbeing.org/programs/the-inner-life-of-social-change-ruby-sales/.

"Tuesday's Broken." Tuesday's Broken Lyrics. https://www.lyrics.com/lyric/35019782/Sugarland/Tuesday's Broken.

Ugolino, Brother. *The Little Flowers of St. Francis.* Grand Rapids: Christian Classics Ethereal Library, 1930.

Valli, Katja, Robert J. Hoss and Robert P. Gongloff. *Dreams Understanding Biology, Psychology, and Culture.* Santa Barbara, CA: Greenwood, an imprint of ABC-CLIO,LLC, 2019.

Ware, Bronnie. "Bronnie Ware." *Bronnie Ware* (blog). https://bronnieware.com/blog/regrets-of-the-dying/.

Wells, Bryan and Ronald N. Miller. *A Place in the Sun lyrics.* Sony/ATV Music Publishing LLC. 1966.

Williamson, Marianne. *A Return to Love: Reflections on the Principles of A Course in Miracles.* New York: HarperColins, 1992.

"20 Quotes from the Ancient Scriptures of Hinduism." *Become an Ordained Interfaith Chaplain or Community Minister*, August 9, 2018. https://chaplaincyinstitute.org/portfolio-items/20-quotes-from-the-ancient-scriptures-of-hinduism/.

New City Press

New City Press is one of more than 20 publishing houses sponsored by the Focolare, a movement founded by Chiara Lubich to help bring about the realization of Jesus' prayer: "That all may be one" (John 17:21). In view of that goal, New City Press publishes books and resources that enrich the lives of people and help all to strive toward the unity of the entire human family. We are a member of the Association of Catholic Publishers.

www.newcitypress.com
202 Comforter Blvd.
Hyde Park, New York

Periodicals
Living City Magazine
www.livingcitymagazine.com

For discounts and promotions go to www.newcitypress.com and join our email list.